WordPress 4.0 Site Blueprints

Second Edition

Create a variety of exciting sites for e-commerce, networking, video streaming, and more using WordPress

Rachel McCollin

open source
community experience distilled

PUBLISHING

BIRMINGHAM - MUMBAI

WordPress 4.0 Site Blueprints
Second Edition

First published: August 2010

Second edition: September 2015

Production reference: 1210915

Published by Packt Publishing Ltd.
Livery Place
35 Livery Street
Birmingham B3 2PB, UK.

ISBN 978-1-78439-796-8

www.packtpub.com

Credits

Author
Rachel McCollin

Reviewers
Felix Arntz
David Kryzaniak
Mario Peshev
Dan Purdy

Commissioning Editor
Dipika Gaonkar

Acquisition Editors
Ruchita Bhansali
Llewellyn Rozario

Content Development Editor
Neeshma Ramakrishnan

Technical Editor
Ankita Thakur

Copy Editor
Swati Priya

Project Coordinator
Shweta H. Birwatkar

Proofreader
Safis Editing

Indexer
Mariammal Chettiyar

Production Coordinator
Arvindkumar Gupta

Cover Work
Arvindkumar Gupta

About the Author

Rachel McCollin is an experienced WordPress developer and writer with a reputation for making difficult technical subjects easy to understand. She's been building WordPress sites for clients since 2010, and this is her fourth book on the technology. She's a regular writer for some of the most influential web design and development websites and her writing has helped thousands of people learn how to get started with WordPress and gain more from it.

About the Reviewers

Felix Arntz is a web developer who specializes in WordPress development with a focus on complex web applications, helpful plugins, and backend. In 2012, he started his business, Leaves Webdesign, to provide WordPress solutions for various clients around the world, especially in the U.S. and Germany. He also develops plugins for the WordPress plugin repository.

Besides his work, he is studying applied computer science at the Ruhr Universität Bochum in Germany and looking forward to receiving his degree in early 2016. When he is not coding, he pursues his passion for making music and playing the piano. He also loves going out and enjoying the beautiful city he lives in, playing soccer, and going to the gym. He is also a movie geek and drinks a lot of Mountain Dew.

Having never worked on any book before, he thoroughly enjoyed reviewing this book and is looking forward to help improving books on the same technology in future.

David Kryzaniak is a web application developer at Fox World Travel in Oshkosh, Wisconsin. He holds a BS in information science from the University of Wisconsin, Green Bay. While he is primarily a PHP developer, he tends to do a lot of frontend coding (CSS, JavaScript, and responsive web design) too. He spends a lot of his free time working on both freelance and open source WordPress projects. You can find out more about him at `https://davekz.com`.

Mario Peshev is the founder of and a WordPress architect at DevriX, a distributed WordPress development agency. He has been building software solutions with PHP, Java, and Python for more than 10 years now.

In addition to his technical background, he is an international speaker and a seasoned trainer with over 10,000 hours on stage. He has conducted training courses on web and database development and security in companies and organizations such as CERN, Saudi Aramco, VMware, and Software AG.

He is currently leading a team of WordPress engineers that builds high-end solutions using the technology. With several WordPress-driven SaaS solutions behind it, the team specializes in complex multisite projects and business-specific solutions based on the popular platform. As a WordPress contributor and active community member, he is often involved with international WordPress or web development events.

Dan Purdy started his career as a technical engineer for a top London recording studio. It was during this time that he started working with WordPress as a blogging tool for his personal projects.

Currently working for a digital innovation agency in Shoreditch, London, as a senior frontend developer, he continues to build sites with WordPress while working on a variety of projects—from product prototypes and e-commerce sites to enterprise-level web applications.

He was also the technical reviewer for *Raspberry Pi Gaming, Second Edition, Packt Publishing*.

www.PacktPub.com

Support files, eBooks, discount offers, and more

For support files and downloads related to your book, please visit www.PacktPub.com.

Did you know that Packt offers eBook versions of every book published, with PDF and ePub files available? You can upgrade to the eBook version at www.PacktPub.com and as a print book customer, you are entitled to a discount on the eBook copy. Get in touch with us at service@packtpub.com for more details.

At www.PacktPub.com, you can also read a collection of free technical articles, sign up for a range of free newsletters and receive exclusive discounts and offers on Packt books and eBooks.

https://www2.packtpub.com/books/subscription/packtlib

Do you need instant solutions to your IT questions? PacktLib is Packt's online digital book library. Here, you can search, access, and read Packt's entire library of books.

Why subscribe?

- Fully searchable across every book published by Packt
- Copy and paste, print, and bookmark content
- On demand and accessible via a web browser

Free access for Packt account holders

If you have an account with Packt at www.PacktPub.com, you can use this to access PacktLib today and view 9 entirely free books. Simply use your login credentials for immediate access.

Table of Contents

Preface

WordPress is now by far the most popular content management system (CMS) with over a quarter of the total websites on the Web running on it. Originally, it was developed as a blogging platform, but it can do much more than that.

If you're like the millions of people who want to use WordPress to sell products, reach an audience, showcase your work, or communicate with a team, among other things, this book is for you. In each chapter, I've used WordPress and shown you how to set up a site that does exactly that.

You don't need to write code to follow the majority of the chapters; all you need is some familiarity with WordPress and adding content to it and the enthusiasm to create a great website.

So what are you waiting for? Here you go for your fantastic website!

What this book covers

Chapter 1, Migrating a Static Site to WordPress, explains how to move an existing site to WordPress and import content from your old site to your new WordPress site.

Chapter 2, Creating a Social Media Site, shows how to use BuddyPress to create a networking site for a community of users.

Chapter 3, Creating a Network of Sites, shows how to create a WordPress Multisite network that will allow users to create their own blog, such as https://wordpress.com/ or http://edublogs.org/.

Chapter 4, Creating an E-commerce Site, explains how to use the free WooCommerce plugin to create an e-commerce site and add real and virtual products to it for sale.

Chapter 5, Creating a Video Streaming Site, shows how to use WordPress to set up and manage a video streaming site, which automatically updates from your own YouTube channel.

Chapter 6, Creating a Review Site, explains how to create a WordPress site that lets users post reviews on products or services.

Chapter 7, Creating a Jobs Board, shows how to use WordPress to create a jobs board so that users can post job advertisements and apply for jobs.

Chapter 8, Creating a Team Communications Site, shows you how to use the free P2 theme to create a site for the members of a team to communicate with the team and update each other on the progress of a project.

Chapter 9, Creating a Gallery Site, explains how to build a WordPress site using a suitable theme and the popular NextGEN Gallery plugin to display images.

Chapter 10, Creating a Membership Site, shows how to create a site that allows users to register as members and view content, which only the registered members have access to.

What you need for this book

To use this book, you will need:

- One or more development sites (one per chapter) running the latest version of WordPress
- Administrator access to your WordPress sites
- Access to files in your site via FTP or cPanel
- A text editor or code editor

Who this book is for

WordPress 4.0 Site Blueprints, Second Edition, is suitable for both new and experienced WordPress users. You don't need to be a PHP developer or have ever created a WordPress theme or plugin; instead, the book will help you use themes and plugins (all free) to create a wide range of sites. Familiarity with the WordPress interface will help you, but you don't need to be able to write code.

Conventions

In this book, you will find a number of text styles that distinguish between different kinds of information. Here are some examples of these styles and an explanation of their meaning.

Code words in text, database table names, folder names, filenames, file extensions, pathnames, dummy URLs, user input, and Twitter handles are shown as follows: "Sometimes, your `wp-content` directory will have some extra folders, for example, if a plugin adds one."

A block of code is set as follows:

```
require ('./wp-blog-header.php')
```

New terms and **important words** are shown in bold. Words that you see on the screen, for example, in menus or dialog boxes, appear in the text like this: "Click on the **Databases** tab."

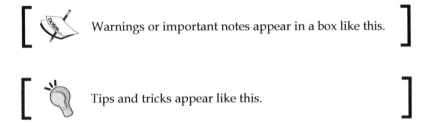

Warnings or important notes appear in a box like this.

Tips and tricks appear like this.

Reader feedback

Feedback from our readers is always welcome. Let us know what you think about this book—what you liked or disliked. Reader feedback is important for us as it helps us develop titles that you will really get the most out of.

To send us general feedback, simply e-mail `feedback@packtpub.com`, and mention the book's title in the subject of your message.

If there is a topic that you have expertise in and you are interested in either writing or contributing to a book, see our author guide at `www.packtpub.com/authors`.

Customer support

Now that you are the proud owner of a Packt book, we have a number of things to help you to get the most from your purchase.

Downloading the color images of this book

We also provide you with a PDF file that has color images of the screenshots/diagrams used in this book. The color images will help you better understand the changes in the output. You can download this file from: `https://www.packtpub.com/sites/default/files/downloads/7968OS_ColorImages.pdf`.

Errata

Although we have taken every care to ensure the accuracy of our content, mistakes do happen. If you find a mistake in one of our books—maybe a mistake in the text or the code—we would be grateful if you could report this to us. By doing so, you can save other readers from frustration and help us improve subsequent versions of this book. If you find any errata, please report them by visiting `http://www.packtpub.com/submit-errata`, selecting your book, clicking on the **Errata Submission Form** link, and entering the details of your errata. Once your errata are verified, your submission will be accepted and the errata will be uploaded to our website or added to any list of existing errata under the Errata section of that title.

To view the previously submitted errata, go to `https://www.packtpub.com/books/content/support` and enter the name of the book in the search field. The required information will appear under the **Errata** section.

Piracy

Piracy of copyrighted material on the Internet is an ongoing problem across all media. At Packt, we take the protection of our copyright and licenses very seriously. If you come across any illegal copies of our works in any form on the Internet, please provide us with the location address or website name immediately so that we can pursue a remedy.

Please contact us at `copyright@packtpub.com` with a link to the suspected pirated material.

We appreciate your help in protecting our authors and our ability to bring you valuable content.

Questions

If you have a problem with any aspect of this book, you can contact us at `questions@packtpub.com`, and we will do our best to address the problem.

1
Migrating a Static Site to WordPress

Many people come to WordPress after some experience of creating static sites using HTML and CSS; in fact, this is what happened to me. I had been building static sites for a while and wanted to start developing with **content management system (CMS)**, which would make it easy for me to import existing static sites and update them using the CMS interface.

The great news is that WordPress makes it possible for you to do this. In this chapter, you'll learn how to move your old site to WordPress as well as gain an understanding of how WordPress works and the benefits of using it. We'll cover these topics:

- The difference between a WordPress site and a static site
- How WordPress is structured and how it stores your site's content and design information
- How to install WordPress on your server and set it up while keeping your old site live
- How to choose and install a theme
- How to add content to your new WordPress site, including importing content from your old site and adding new posts and pages
- Installing plugins to add extra functionality
- Launching your site once it is ready

So let's get started!

In this book, you'll learn how to download and activate a theme that will give your site its styling and layout. If you want to learn how to take your static site and develop your own theme-based on the code in your HTML files, I recommend *WordPress Theme Development Beginner's Guide, Packt Publishing*.

WordPress versus static sites – the differences

If you've built static sites before, you'll know that they consist of a number of files that you upload to your server. These will include:

- HTML files
- One or more CSS files (referred to as style sheets)
- Possibly JavaScript files if you're running sliders or other dynamic elements on your site

Your WordPress site will include different file types and it will also include a database, which is where your content will be stored.

The main elements of a WordPress site are:

- The files running WordPress itself. These are mainly PHP files.
- The files in your site's theme, including one CSS file (occasionally more) and a number of PHP files.
- The files in any plugins you install. These will always include PHP files but may also include CSS and JavaScript files.
- Files you upload to your site, including images and PDF files.
- Your site's database, which will include a number of tables storing your content and site settings.

You'll learn more about these and what they do in the next section.

Understanding how WordPress stores content

Having read the list of files contained in a WordPress site, you may be feeling quite daunted! But the good news is that you don't need to think about the files I've listed here as WordPress does the thinking for you.

So, let's take a look at the contents of a WordPress site in more detail.

WordPress files

When you install WordPress, a number of files are uploaded to your server. The good news is that you don't need to do anything to these files; in fact, you shouldn't. If you edit these files (referred to as the core files), any changes you make will be lost when you install the next WordPress update.

Later in this chapter, you'll learn how to install WordPress. Once you've done that, you can ignore the core files. Phew!

Theme and plugin files and uploads

The next set of files is stored in the `wp-content` directory, inside your WordPress installation. This directory will normally look similar to this:

Name ▼	Size	Date
▶ 📁 uploads	--	15 Jan 2015 20:46
▶ 📁 themes	--	15 Jan 2015 21:02
▶ 📁 plugins	--	15 Jan 2015 23:22
📄 index.php	28 B	15 Jan 2015 14:39

Fig 1.1: The wp-content directory

Let's take a look at the file types:

- `themes`: When you create your site, you will need to install a theme, which is what will give your site its design and layout and possibly, some extra features too, depending on the theme. There are thousands of themes available for you to download and use on your site, and a lot of them are free. WordPress stores the files for your theme in the `themes` folder, with each theme having its own folder. You'll never need to open these files or edit them.

- `plugins`: These are extra packages you install in your site to add more functionality. There are thousands of plugins available, and like themes, a lot of them are free. Later in this chapter, you'll learn how to install and configure plugins on your site. Again, the good news is that you don't have to worry about these files; WordPress will do the work for you.

- `uploads`: This folder contains all of the images and other media that you upload to your site. When you first install WordPress you might not have this folder yet, as it's automatically created the first time you upload media to your site. You don't actually upload these directly to this folder; instead, you use the WordPress interface to upload them and then WordPress stores them in the correct place for you. It is another example of WordPress making your life easier! Later in this chapter, you'll learn how to upload an image and insert it in a page on your site.

Sometimes, your `wp-content` directory will have some extra folders, for example, if a plugin adds one. Don't worry if that happens, just leave them alone!

Database

The final piece in the jigsaw is the database. This is where all of your content is stored—your posts, pages, and any settings you've made on your site.

The main benefit of using a database is that it keeps your content and your design separate. As your site grows, this makes your life much easier because you don't have to directly edit HTML files if you want to make changes to your site. The parts of each page that are the same across the site (for example, the header, footer, and sidebars) are kept separate from content, meaning if you want to change them you only have to do it once.

Everything you may need to do with your WordPress site can be done via the WordPress administration screens; you never need to touch the code. If you're not a techie, this will be a very good news!

Installing WordPress

Now that you understand how WordPress works, you're probably itching to get started! So, let's start by installing WordPress. There are two ways to do this:

- Using an installer such as Softaculous or Fantastico, which may be provided by your hosting company
- Directly installing WordPress using the Famous 5 Minute Install

Let's start with the easier way, which is to use an installer.

Installing WordPress using an installer

If your hosting provider gives you access to an installer, it will probably be accessible via your hosting dashboard or cPanel, which is a dashboard many hosting providers give you to manage your site.

 The exact way this looks and where you find it will vary from host to host, so your screen will probably look slightly different from what you see here, but the process is much the same.

My hosting provider includes a link in its control panel called **Web Apps**. Yours might be called Fantastico, Softaculous, or something else. If you're unsure, check with your hosting company and ask them if they provide a WordPress installer.

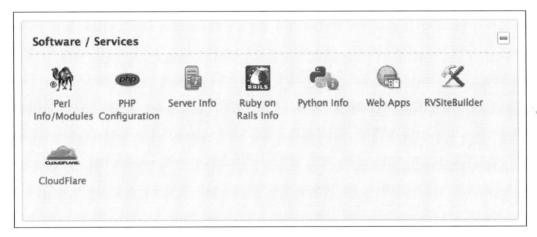

Fig 1.2: Accessing an installer

When I open this, I see a list of the web apps available to me, including WordPress:

Fig 1.3: Choosing WordPress in the installer

These are the steps you need to follow now:

1. Click on **WordPress** and then on **Install Now**.

2. You will be presented with a list of fields to complete. Fill them out as follows:
   - **Prefix**: I prefer to use just http:// as the www really isn't necessary these days.
   - **Domain**: This will already be filled out with your domain name; leave it as it is.
   - **Directory**: If you add something here, WordPress will be installed in a subdirectory of your site and not in your root directory. If you already have a static site running on this domain, using a subdirectory will mean that your static site will still work while you install and set up WordPress. If not, it's easier to leave this empty. You'll learn later in this chapter how to manage your old site while you're setting up WordPress.

- ◦ **Database Name**: You can leave this as it is or change it to something that's more memorable to you. If you're not going to be working on your database, just leave it alone.

- ◦ **Table Prefix**: Leave this as wp_.

- ◦ **Site Name**: This is where you enter your site's title.

- ◦ **Site Description**: This is where you enter your description or strapline. Most themes will display this below the title at the top of your pages. If you don't have a description, leave this blank.

- ◦ **Enable Multisite**: If this is offered by your installer, leave it unchecked.

- ◦ **Admin Username**: The default is admin, but for security reasons, you should change this to something unique and memorable for you.

- ◦ **Admin Password**: Enter your password twice for logging in to your site. Be sure to make it secure, including uppercase letters, numbers, and other characters.

- ◦ **Admin Email**: Enter your e-mail address.

- ◦ **Select Language**: If this is an option, select your language if it isn't English.

- ◦ **Select Plugins**: This isn't offered by all installers, so you may not see it. I leave this blank, preferring to install plugins later on.

- ◦ **Email recipient**: If you add your e-mail address here, you will receive an e-mail with details of your new WordPress installation, including a link to the admin screens.

 Some installers offer a backup option, which is a good idea to select if available. It's also a good idea to use a backup plugin in your site too. For a review of some of the best backup plugins, visit http://premium.wpmudev.org/blog/premium-freemium-wordpress-backup-plugins/.

Here, you can see an example for the installation I'm setting up:

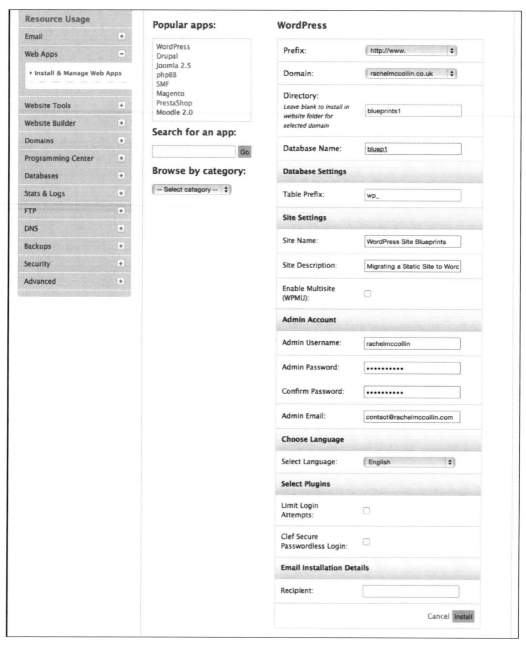

Fig 1.4: Enter your site details

Once you've entered your details, click on **Install** and the installer will do its work. You will see a screen with a link to your new site and to the admin screens. Well done!

But what do you do if your hosting provider doesn't give you access to an installer? That's where manual installation comes in.

Installing WordPress manually

Installing WordPress manually takes a little longer, but isn't difficult as long as you know the steps to take. You'll need to learn how to do this if your hosting company doesn't provide an installer or if you want to install WordPress locally on your PC or Mac. This can be useful for working on a development site, where you're creating a dummy version of the site before you launch it to the world.

If you want to install WordPress on your local machine, the process is very similar to the one here, but you'll also need to install an app such as MAMP (for Mac and Windows) or XAMPP (for Mac, Windows, or Linux). You can find instructions at `http://codex.wordpress.org/Installing_WordPress_Locally_on_Your_Mac_With_MAMP` and `http://premium.wpmudev.org/blog/how-to-install-wordpress-locally-for-pcwindows-with-xampp/`. For a guide to migrating your site to the live site once you're happy with it, refer to `http://code.tutsplus.com/tutorials/migrating-a-wordpress-site-from-a-local-server-to-production--wp-26`.

Installing WordPress manually consists of four steps:

* Downloading the WordPress files
* Creating a database on your web server
* Uploading the WordPress files to your server
* Running the WordPress installation script by accessing the URL for your site in your browser

Let's work through each of those steps in turn.

Downloading the WordPress files

To download the WordPress files, follow these steps:

1. Go to `https://wordpress.org/download/` and click on the **Download** button to download the files.
2. This will download a `.zip` file to your computer. Unzip this.

Creating a database on your server using phpMyAdmin

Your site will need a database to hold all of your content. WordPress doesn't create this for you; you'll have to do it yourself.

1. In your hosting provider's dashboard or in cPanel, go to phpMyAdmin. If you can't find this, ask your hosting provider; they might have a different way to create a database, such as using a wizard.

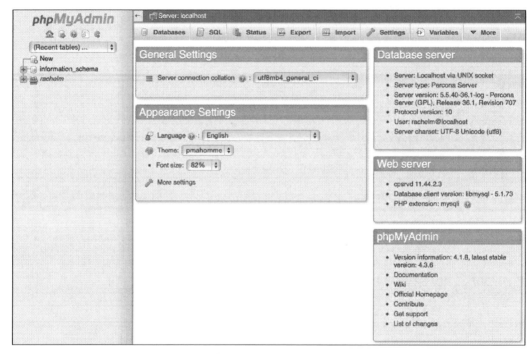

Fig 1.5: The phpMyAdmin home screen

2. Click on the **Databases** tab.

3. You will see a field labeled **Create a new database**. Type the name of your database in this field. Make a note of this as you'll need it again later.

4. Click on **OK**.

You now have an empty database set up. The next step is to upload WordPress.

 Some hosting providers don't let you create databases in phpMyAdmin; you have to do it in your hosting dashboard instead. If this is the case, follow the instructions given by your hosting provider.

Uploading WordPress to your server

To upload WordPress, you'll need an FTP client or a code editing program with FTP built in. I tend to use Coda (`http://panic.com/coda/`), which is a code editor for the Mac, or FileZilla (`https://filezilla-project.org`), which is a free FTP client.

1. In your FTP client or code editor, display your `Downloads` folder locally and the files on your remote server.

2. If you already have a static site on your server and want to keep it running while you create your new site, create a folder inside your `public_html` folder. I'm creating a folder called `blueprints1`, as you can see in the following screenshot. If you don't have an existing site, you can skip this step.

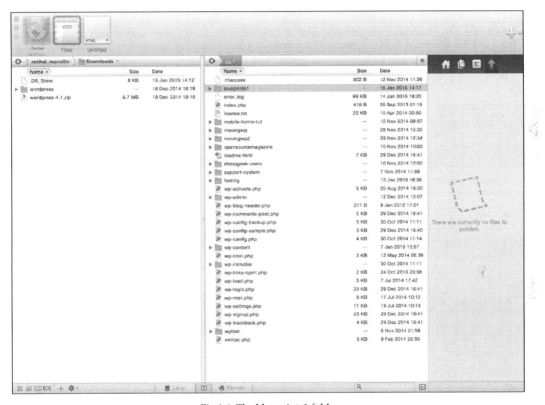

Fig 1.6: The blueprints1 folder

3. Now copy the contents of the `wordpress` folder from your `Downloads` folder to the folder you've created. If you haven't created a folder, copy it to the `public_html` folder. Don't copy the `wordpress` folder, copy its contents.

4. Make yourself a coffee while you wait for the files to upload!

Now that you have a database and the WordPress files uploaded, you just need to activate the WordPress installation script by visiting your new site's URL in your browser.

Activating the WordPress installation script

To activate the installation script, you'll need to perform the following steps in your browser:

1. In your browser of choice, type in the URL for your new site. Remember that if you've created a folder for your site, it will be `http://yourdomain.com/folder`, where `folder` is the name of your new folder and `yourdomain.com` is your domain name.

2. You will be presented with the first of the installation screens, where you choose your language. Select your language and click on **Continue**.

3. The next screen tells you what's coming up. Give it a quick read (and don't worry!) and click on **Let's go!**.

4. The following screen is where you need to give WordPress some information about your database so that it can access it. Input the following:

   ○ **Database Name**: Enter the name you gave your database earlier

   ○ **User Name**: Enter the username you created for your database earlier

   ○ **Password**: Enter the password you assigned to your new username

   ○ **Database Host**: Leave this as **localhost** (unless your hosting provider uses a different hostname)

   ○ **Table Prefix**: Leave this as **wp_**

You can see what I've entered in the following screenshot:

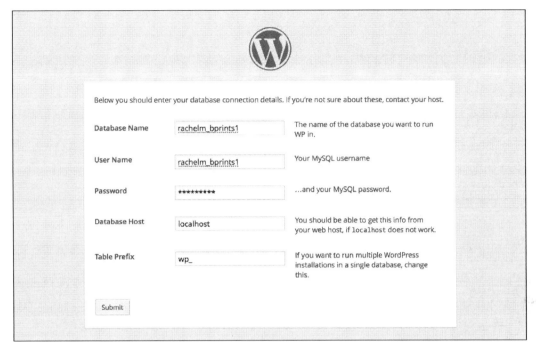

Fig 1.7: Entering your database details to install WordPress

5. You'll now see a screen congratulating you on getting this far. Click on the **Run the install** button to continue.

6. You're nearly there! All that's left is to enter your site details on the next screen:

    ° **Site Title**: Enter the name of your site.

    ° **Username**: Enter your username for logging in to your site (which is different form your database username—don't use the same username as this will make your site less secure).

    ° **Password twice**: Enter the password you want to use to log in.

    ° **Your Email**: Enter your e-mail address for notifications.

    ° **Privacy**: Uncheck this for now as this is a development site and you don't want search engines finding it just yet. Don't forget to go back and check the box when you launch the site, otherwise you won't get picked up by Google.

Here's what I've added:

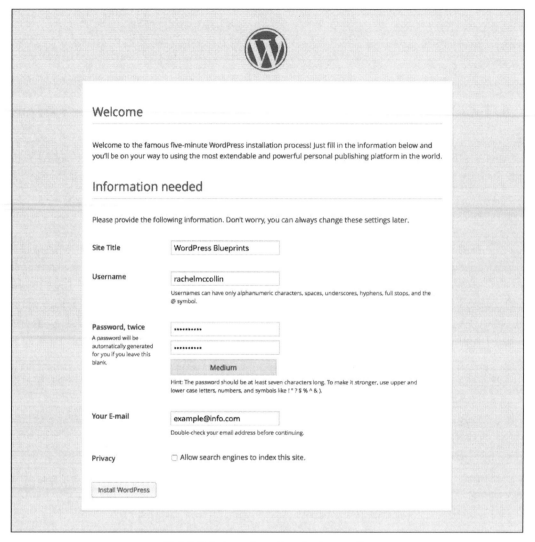

Fig 1.8: Entering information about your site

7. Next, you'll see the success screen. Click on the **Log in** button to access your new site.

8. Now simply log in with your username and password and you'll be able to start administering your site.

The WordPress Dashboard and administration screens

Now that you've installed WordPress (whichever method you used) and logged in, you'll see the **Dashboard** screen. If you can see this screen, you've done everything correctly. Well done!

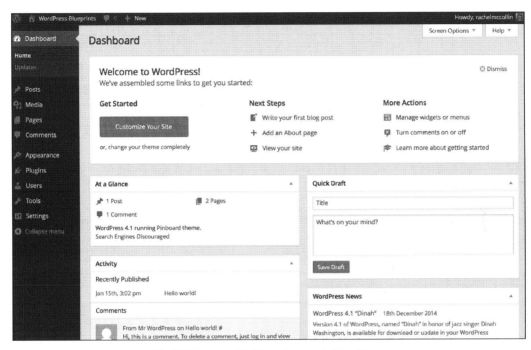

Fig 1.9: The main Dashboard screen in WordPress

But before you start configuring your site and adding content to it, let's take a moment to look at how this affects your old site.

Keeping your old site live while setting WordPress up

In the previous section, I mentioned installing WordPress in a subdirectory if you have an existing static site that you want to keep live while you create your new one.

Let's look at how this works:

1. You install WordPress in a subdirectory, which has a different name from any of the pages in your site (if you have an HTML file with the same name as your subdirectory, the browser might go to the WordPress installation instead of that HTML page when a link to it is clicked).

2. You uncheck the box, allowing search engines to index your site so that people won't stumble upon it when it's not ready. If you missed this step, you can make the change in the WordPress admin. Simply go to **Settings | Reading** and click on the **Search Engine Visibility** checkbox. Then, click on **Save Changes**. While WordPress does give you a warning that this is up to the search engines, in my experience, they do honor this and your site won't get found.

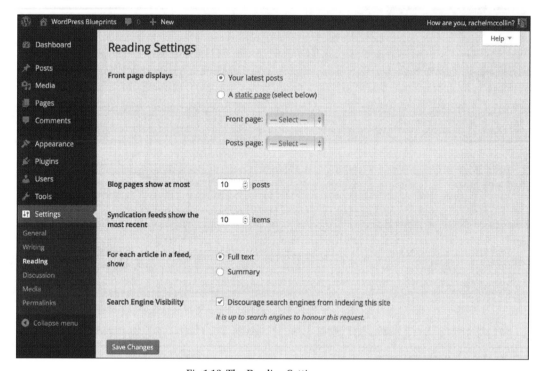

Fig 1.10: The Reading Settings screen

3. Once your new site is ready, you don't need to move it to the root directory; you just make a couple of small edits to the files and settings, and this tells WordPress that the site is in a subdirectory. We'll look at this later on in the chapter once your site is set up.

Installing a theme

Congratulations, you've now got a working WordPress site! It comes with the default theme bundled, which, at the time of writing this book, is **Twenty Fifteen**. While this is a good theme, you probably want to give your site a more bespoke design, so the next step is to find and install a suitable theme from the WordPress theme repository.

Introducing the WordPress theme repository

The WordPress theme repository, at `https://wordpress.org/themes/`, contains thousands of themes that you can download for free and use on your site. They vary hugely in terms of their design and the kind of sites they're suited to, but there's a good chance that there'll be one that works for you.

To install a theme, you don't have to go to the WordPress site and manually download it; instead, you can use the theme's screen in your WordPress admin, which you'll learn next.

Choosing a theme

With so many themes to choose from, where do you start? The first thing is to identify a set of keywords to use for searching that may include one or more of the following:

- Colors
- Layout details such as fixed, fluid, responsive, or the number of columns
- Features such as accessibility or featured images
- A subject (the type of site you're running)

Let's try finding a theme by following these steps:

1. Go to **Appearance | Themes** and then click on the **Add New** button. This will open the theme repository in your admin screen.

2. Click on the **Feature Filter** button. This will give you a screen full of checkboxes that you can tick to select keywords and filter the themes you can choose from.

3. If you want your new site to look as similar as possible to your old one, or you have brand colors that you need to use, it makes sense to use **Colors** and **Layout** keywords. Add others as needed to filter down the list of themes.

4. Once you've ticked all the checkboxes you want, scroll back up and click on **Apply Filters**. WordPress will then display the themes that have your keywords applied to them:

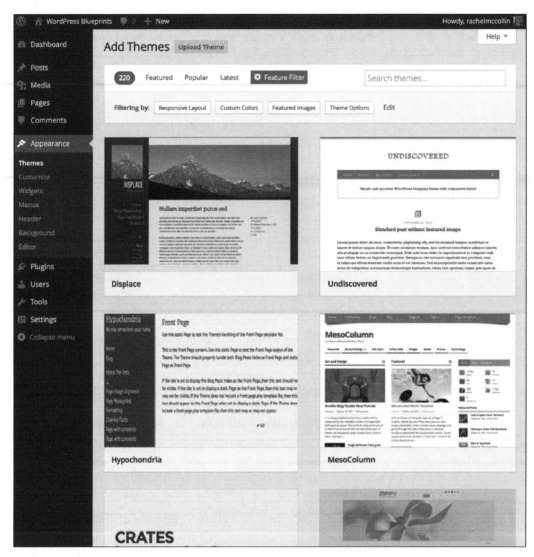

Fig 1.11: A filtered list of themes

5. Scroll down the themes on display and choose the one that you like the look of. Hover over it with your mouse and click on **Preview** to have a look at it or **Install** to install it. Installing it won't do any harm; if you don't like it, you can always uninstall it afterwards.

6. Once you've installed your theme, you'll see a screen telling you that it's successfully installed. It still isn't running on your site yet; to make this happen, click on the **Activate** link.

Next, we'll learn how to customize a theme for our own needs and change its settings.

Customizing your theme using the theme customizer

The theme customizer is a great WordPress feature that lets you make tweaks to a theme and see what difference they make without saving your changes, so it won't be visible to anyone visiting your site until you're ready.

Different themes offer different customization options, which vary from just editing the title and description to more comprehensive options such as customizing colors and layout. You can also edit widgets from the customizer.

I'm going to use a theme called **Pinboard**, which is responsive for mobile devices and offers the option to customize colors and the header and background image. This means I can create a bespoke site meeting my needs.

To install the theme and customize it, follow these steps:

1. Click on **Appearance** to go to the **Themes** screen and click on **Add New**.

2. In the **Search themes...** box, type `Pinboard` and hit the *Enter* key.

3. WordPress will display the **Pinboard** theme for you. Hover over it with your mouse and click on the **Install** button.

4. When you see the installation success screen, click on **Activate**.

5. Next, in the **Themes** screen (click on **Appearance** if it isn't already open), click on the **Customize** button for the **Pinboard** theme.

6. This will open the theme customizer:

Fig 1.12: The theme customizer

7. Start by editing the background image. Click on the **Background Image** link to the left. To remove the wood graphic, click on the **Remove** button.

8. Click on the **Colors** link on the left and select **Background color**. Choose a color using the color picker. I'm choosing white, which will look quite nondescript for now, but will be better once I've made some other changes. Note that you can click on a color or type in the hexadecimal code.

9. Finally, click on the **Save & Publish** button to save your changes.

Hexadecimal codes are codes made up of six letters and numbers which tell a browser what color an element is. They are always preceded by a # and are used in HTML and CSS files to define the color of backgrounds, text, and more. For more on hexadecimal codes, visit http://en.wikipedia.org/wiki/Web_colors.

We're not going to edit any more using the theme customizer because this theme has extensive options screens, which let us do more. Some themes have more options in the theme customizer and don't use separate options screens; it all depends on the way the theme has been designed.

Important: If you want to edit your theme's code, do this using a code editor. Never use the editor that you can access via **Appearance | Editor**. Using this means, you can't undo your changes and could break your site. So, avoid!

Let's take a quick look at how the site is looking with this theme. To view your site, click on the link in the admin bar at the top of the screen with the title of your site; in my case, it's **WordPress Blueprints**.

Here's the site:

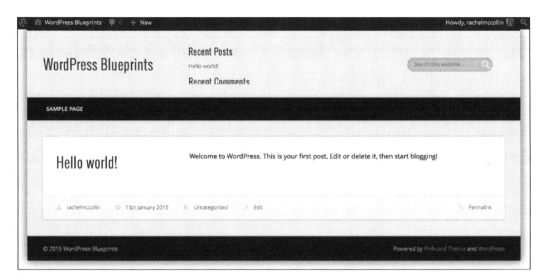

Fig 1.13: The site with the Pinboard theme activated

Customizing your theme via the Themes options screens

This theme has multiple options screens, which we can use to make more changes. Not all themes will have these; it depends on the features that the developer has added.

Customizing colors

Let's make some changes in colors by following these steps:

1. Go back to the admin screens by clicking on your site's name in the admin bar again.
2. Click on **Appearance | Theme Options** to open the theme options screens.

3. Click on the **Design** tab. You'll be presented with a range of color pickers to help you define the colors in your site; either pick a color or input the hexadecimal code for your color.

4. Tweak some of the colors, trying to stick to a palette of colors that work well together. I'm using a palette of blues.

5. Click on the **Save Settings** button and view your site. Here's how mine looks:

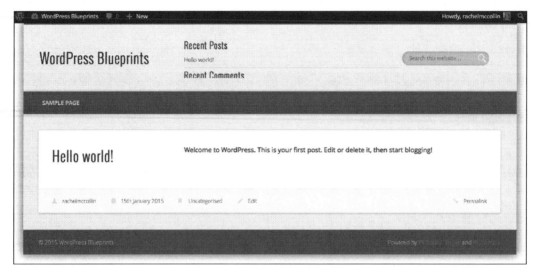

Fig 1.14: The site with colors adjusted

6. Repeat steps 3 to 5 until you're happy with your color scheme.

Customizing fonts

One of my favorite features of this theme is the fact that you can customize not just colors, but fonts too, a feature which not many themes have. So let's do this by following these steps:

1. Go to **Appearance | Theme Options** and click on the **Typography** tab.

2. There are three dropdown lists for fonts—**Default Font Family**, **Headings Font family**, and **Body Copy Font Family**.

3. Select a font you like for each. I recommend sticking to a simple, legible font for body copy, and making the heading font more interesting.

4. Scroll down to the **Font Sizes** options and make any changes you need for your design. Here, you can copy the font sizing that you used on your old site, if you want a similar look and feel.

5. Next, scroll down to the **Colors** options and make changes to the text colors. I'm making some changes to tie in with the changes I already made to the background colors.

6. Click on the **Save Settings** button and view your site. Here's how mine looks:

Fig 1.15: The site with font changes applied

7. Repeat steps 2 to 6 until you're happy.

 If you've been making lots of changes quickly, you might find that they don't all show up. If things aren't working as you expect, just save your changes and refresh the screen.

I'm just going to leave it at this for now, but if you want, you can explore all of the **Themes** options screens and make more changes. Now that we've done some work on the design, it's time to tweak your site's settings.

Adjusting your site's settings

Before adding content, you'll need to adjust some site settings for comments, reading, and permalinks. Follow these steps:

1. Go to **Settings | Discussion**. Make adjustments to the discussion settings according to your site's needs. You may or may not want to allow comments. If you do this now, it will apply to all the new posts and pages you add, and that is why it's a good idea to do it early.

2. Click on the **Save Changes** button.

3. Go to **Settings | Permalinks**. The default setting for **Permalinks** gives your site the URLs, which aren't very friendly to search engines or human beings. Select another option depending on how your site will be structured. For a site consisting of mainly static pages, I would use the **Post name** option as it's good for SEO.

4. Click on **Save Changes**. You'll now find that if you visit a page on your site, the URL is much more sensible.

 If you're using WordPress Version 4.2 or later, the so-called "pretty permalinks" will be set up as the default, so you may be able to skip this step.

5. Go to **Settings | Reading**. Here you can select whether your home page will be a static page or a list of your latest blog posts:

    ◦ To use a static page, select the **A static page** radio button and then select the page you want to use. If you also want to display posts in a blog page elsewhere, you'll need to create an empty page for that and select it in the **Posts page** drop-down box. Note that you may need to come back to this once you've created your home page.

    ◦ To use a list of your latest posts, click on the **Your latest posts** radio button. How these are displayed on your home page will depend on your theme.

6. Click on the **Save Changes** button to save your changes.

Adding content to your site

If you're migrating from a static site, you may well have content from that to import to your new site. Or you may have been running a blog or site on another platform whose content you want to import.

Before we can start importing content, you need to know what kinds of content WordPress uses.

Types of content in WordPress

WordPress uses three main content types:

- **Posts**: These are your blog posts or news articles, which you add regularly. You can access them via the **Posts** admin menu.

- **Pages**: These are static pages such as your content page and "about us" page. Your home page could either be a static page or a page listing all of your latest posts (we'll see how to set that up later on).

- **Attachments**: These are images, PDFs, and other media, stored in the `uploads` folder, which we looked at earlier. Each of them also has an entry in the database, giving WordPress metadata about them. You access these via the **Media** menu or by uploading them to your page or post content.

You can also add your own content types using **Custom Post Types**, but we don't need to worry about that in this chapter.

There are three ways of importing content:

- Using the importer tool
- By copying text from your old site
- By copying code from your old site

Let's start with the importer. This won't help you if your old site was built on HTML alone, but will be useful if you were using another CMS or blogging platform.

Importing content with the importer tool

The importer tool automatically imports content from a range of other services. Perform the following steps:

1. Go to **Tools | Import**.

2. Click on the name of the platform you were using for your old blog.

3. WordPress will take you to an installation screen for the plugin, which imports content form that platform. Click on the **Install Now** button.

4. On the successful installation screen, click on the **Activate Plugin & Run Importer** link.

5. Follow the instructions onscreen. Depending on the platform you're importing from, you may have to upload an xml file or sign in to your account on the other platform. There will be multiple screens and you may have the option to import images as well as text.

6. Once you've finished, click on **Posts** in the admin menu to see what posts have been imported. Your old site's content should have been imported to your new site, saving you a lot of work.

Importing content manually

There are two ways to do this—you can copy the text or the code. Copying the text will be easier if you're not used to working with code, but it may be less reliable.

Copying text from your old site

Let's have a go at copying the text from your old site by importing the text first. Follow these steps:

1. First, create a new page or post. If your old site was a small static one, you probably only have pages to copy. Click on **Pages | Add New** to see the page editing screen:

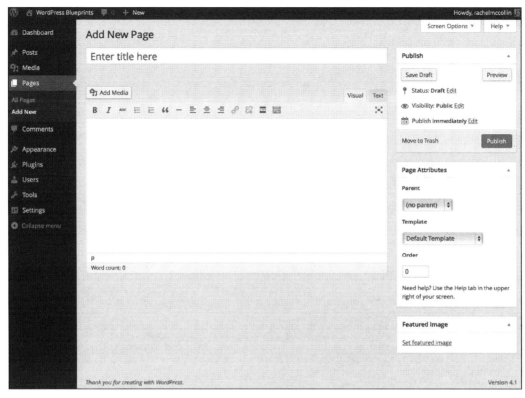

Fig 1.16: The Page editing screen

2. Open your old site in another browser window and open the page you want to copy.

3. Copy the old page's title and type it into the box that says **Enter Title** here.

4. Now, copy the page's content and paste it onto the main page editing pane below the title.

5. Check how it looks. If the layout and styling is a bit of a mess, you might need to start again, copying the code instead.

6. Delete any images. You'll need to upload those to WordPress separately as any images that have copied across will be linking to the image files stored in the old site, which will disappear when you eventually remove that site.

7. Click on the **Publish** button to save your new page.

8. Repeat this for the other pages in your site.

Copying code from your old site

The page editing screen gives you the option to edit the HTML in the page; this means that you can paste HTML from your old site into your new pages by following these steps:

1. Click on **Pages | Add New** to create your new page if you haven't done so already.

2. Type the page title into the title box at the top of the screen.

3. Above the content pane, click on the **Text** tab on the right-hand side.

4. Open the HTML file for the page you want to copy from your old site. Find the HTML for the content and copy it. Don't copy the HTML for the header, sidebar, footer, or page title, or anything from the <head> section of the page. You will probably be copying a lot of text within <p> tags and a few other tags such as <ul> and <img>.

5. Paste this code into the content pane in WordPress.

6. Click on the **Visual** tab to return to the visual editor and see the results of what you've done.

7. Delete any images; you'll need to upload these manually.

8. Tidy up any formatting. You might need to switch between the **Visual** and **Text** tabs if there's any code causing problems. Do this with caution!

9. Click on the **Publish** button to save your new page.

10. Repeat this for the other pages in your site.

Creating new pages and posts

Once you've imported the content from your old site (or if you don't want to do that), you can start creating new pages and posts. To create new pages, simply follow the steps described for copying text from your old site in the preceding section, but instead of copying in the text, type it in manually.

To create a new post, follow these steps:

1. Click on **Posts | Add New**.

2. Type your post's title in the title box and the content in the text editing pane below. Use the formatting toolbar to change styles if needs be.

The formatting toolbar gives you the option to change fonts and colors, but I would strongly advise not to do this. Use the styles provided with your theme and tweak fonts and colors using the **Themes** options screens. This will retain a professional, coherent look to your site.

3. When you're ready, click on the **Publish** button to save your post.

4. If you want to, assign one or more categories or tags to your post by selecting them from the list on the right-hand side or typing in new ones.

5. Keep on doing this. If you want to add a back catalogue of posts, you can amend the publish date for each post in the **Publish** pane by clicking on **Publish** immediately and selecting the date you want to use. This will make your blog look more established than it would if all your posts had today's date!

Uploading images and media

The easiest way to add images and other media is to add them inside your posts or pages. Let's start with images.

Adding images to your posts and pages

WordPress lets you insert images anywhere you want in your post or page content by performing these steps:

1. Open the post or page you want to add an image to and click on the point in the text where you want the image to appear.

2. Click on the **Add Media** tab to open the media upload screen.

3. Click on **Select Files** and select the image file you want to upload.

4. The file will be imported and you'll see it on the screen. Now, work your way through the options on the right-hand side of the screen:

   ° **Title**: This is the name of the image. Leave this as it is or change it to something more meaningful for accessibility and SEO so that it can help when searching media on your site.

   ° **Caption**: Type the caption text here or leave it blank.

   ° **Alt text**: Type in the alternative text for screen readers.

   ° **Description**: Adding a description can help with SEO. It won't be displayed on the page, but may show up in search results.

- ° **Alignment**: Select how you want to the image to be aligned. If you choose **Left** or **Right**, the text will wrap around the image.

- ° **Link To**: Specify if you want visitors to be able to click on the image and go to its file or attachment page, to a custom URL, or if you want no link at all.

- ° **Size**: Select from the default sizes WordPress gives you to choose how big this will appear on the screen.

5. Click on **Insert into page** to insert the image.

6. Your image will now appear in the editing screen, but it might not look very good because your theme's formatting isn't applied in the admin screens. To check how it looks, either click on the **Preview** button to preview without publishing your changes or click on the **Update** button to save your changes and then click on **View** page at the top of the screen. Here's my page with an image added:

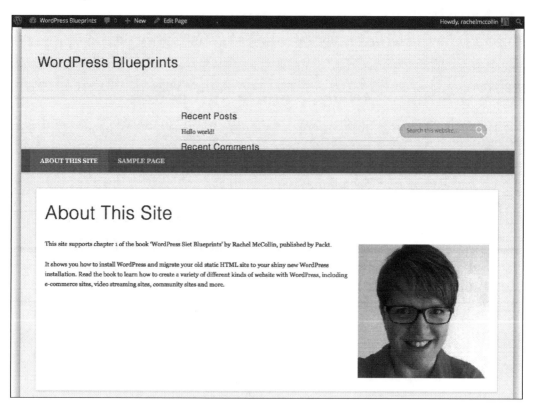

Fig 1.17: The page with a right-aligned image of me!

Adding PDF files to your posts and pages

Adding PDF files is similar to adding images, with some minor differences. Perform these steps:

1. Open your post or page and click on the point in the text where you want the PDF to appear.

2. Click on the **Add Media** button and then **Select Files**.

3. Select the file you want to upload. WordPress will upload it and display an icon for it on the screen:

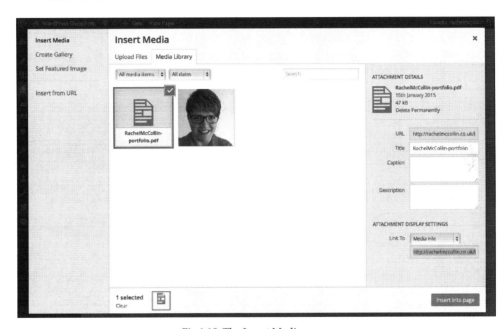

Fig 1.18: The Insert Media screen

4. Complete the options on the right-hand side:

   ° **URL**: Leave this as it is.

   ° **Title**: This is the text that people will click on to download the file. Change this to something that makes sense for visitors.

   ° **Caption**: Leave this blank.

   ° **Description**: Add something here for SEO if you wish.

   ° **Link To**: Choose whether to link to the file itself (my preference) or to an attachment page with the media file in it. I don't like this as it makes the visitor click too many times.

5. Click on **Insert into page**.

To test what you've done, click on the **Update** button and then the **View page** link. My page now has a clickable link to a file:

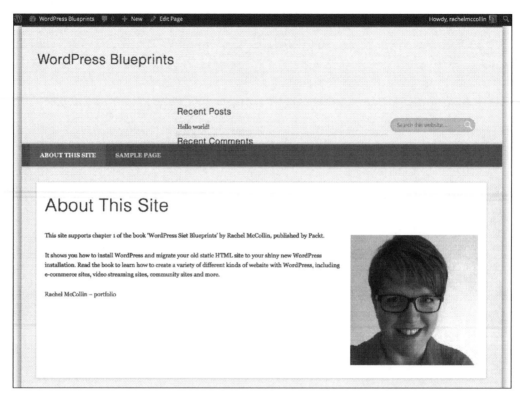

Fig 1.19: My page with an image and a media file

Now, you can repeat this with all of the images and files you want to add to your site.

> WordPress also supports video uploads and streaming videos from other sites. You'll learn about this in *Chapter 5, Creating a Video Streaming Site.*

Setting up navigation menus and widgets

Most themes support navigation menus that you can edit using the WordPress admin screens. This is much easier than coding your menus. They will also support widgets, which are items you can add to widget areas (normally in the footer and sidebar) to display lists of posts, links to other sites, social media feeds and links, and much more.

Let's start by setting up the navigation menu.

Creating the main navigation menu

You can use the **Menus** screen to create one or more navigation menus; sometimes, you might want to add extra smaller menus to your footer, for example, to display links to the popular content. But here, we'll create the main navigation menu by performing these steps:

1. Go to **Appearance | Menus**.

2. Depending on how your theme is set up, you may see a dummy menu displayed with your pages. To create a menu from it, click on **Create Menu**.

3. Click on the **Primary Menu** checkbox below the menu. This will add it to the site's main navigation area.

4. Click on the **Save Menu** button.

5. Now go back to your site's frontend to view your menu:

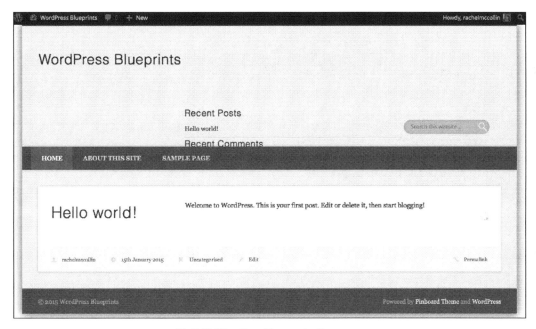

Fig 1.20: The site with a navigation menu

6. Go back to the **Menus** screen to make adjustments to your menu if you need to. You can drag additional posts, pages, and categories (if you've created categories for your posts) on to it.

7. Every time you make changes, remember to click on the **Save Menu** button. WordPress doesn't save changes to the menu in the background.

Adding widgets

Now let's add some widgets. Each theme will have different widget areas, which is where you place your widgets. Normally, you'll find widget areas in the sidebar and footer, but this theme has extra ones, giving more flexibility. Perform these steps:

1. Go to **Appearance | Widgets**.

2. By default, WordPress places a set of widgets in the theme's first widget area. In this theme, the first widget area is in the header, and those widgets look a bit odd there. Remove all of them except the **Search** widget by clicking on the arrow to the right of its box and clicking on **Delete**.

3. Now, drag some widgets into the other widget area, putting them where you think they are appropriate. Think about mirroring the content in your old site where possible. If you want to just insert some text or HTML, you can do this using the **Text** widget. You can add more than one widget to each widget area, but don't go too mad!

Here are my widgets displayed in the **Widgets** screen:

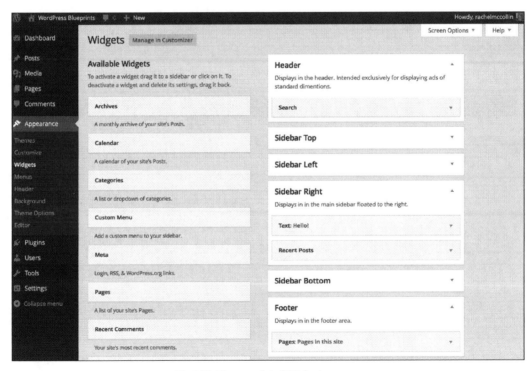

Fig 1.21: The populated Widgets screen

Here they are on my site's home page:

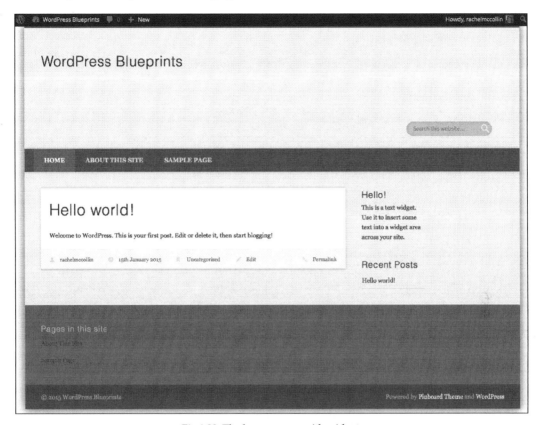

Fig 1.22: The home screen with widgets

Installing plugins

Plugins can do just about any job you can think of, but some of the most common are:

- Widgets to put in your sidebar or footer
- Shortcodes that let you add code into your page without actually writing the code
- Image galleries and slideshows
- Links to external sites, such as social media feeds
- SEO plugins to help you get found by search engines
- Forms plugins to help your visitors get in touch with you
- Performance plugins that will make your site run faster

Let's install a popular SEO plugin called **WordPress SEO** by Yoast:

1. Go to **Plugins | Add New**.

2. In the **Search plugins...** box, type WordPress SEO and hit the *Enter* key.

3. WordPress will display a list of plugins, meeting your search criteria. Find the plugin called WordPress SEO by Yoast and click on the **Install Now** button.

4. When asked whether you're sure you want to install the plugin, click on **OK**.

5. When you see the success screen, click on the **Activate** link.

6. The plugin is now installed and activated on your site.

I'm not going to show you how to configure the plugin as that's outside the scope of this book, but you will find guidance on the plugin website at https://yoast.com/wordpress/plugins/seo/.

Now try installing some more plugins according to your site's needs. We'll be working with lots of plugins in the other chapters of this book, so you'll get to try plenty of them out.

Making your WordPress site live

Once you have all your content in place, have installed and configured any plugins you want to use, and are happy with your widgets and with any customizations you've made to the design, it's time to go live.

If you aren't running your old site on the server still and didn't install WordPress in a subdirectory, this is very simple. Perform these steps:

1. Go to **Settings | Reading**.

2. Uncheck the **Search Engine Visibility** checkbox.

That's it! Search engines can now find your site. You'll need to do a bit more to publicize it, but it's now public. Enjoy!

However, if you still have your static site running, there's a bit more to do:

1. In your FTP client or in File Manager in cPanel, find the folder where the WordPress files are located and find two files—index.php and .htaccess. If you haven't made any changes to permalinks, you won't have an .htaccess file, so just work with index.php.

2. Copy the two files (or one if you don't have `.htaccess`) to the next directory up, that is, `public_html`.

3. Open the copy in `public_html` and find the line that reads as follows:

    ```
    require ('./wp-blog-header.php')
    ```

4. Change it to this:

    ```
    require ('./XXX/wp-blog-header.php'),
    ```

    Here, xxx is the name of your subdirectory.

5. Save the file.

6. Back in the WordPress admin, go to **Settings | General**.

7. Edit the **Site Address** and **WordPress Address** fields so that they read as follows, where `site.com` is your domain and `folder` is the name of your subfolder where WordPress is stored. Change them to the following, making sure you spell everything correctly to avoid redirect loops:

    - ◦ **WordPress address (URL)**: `http://site.com/folder`
    - ◦ **Site Address (URL)**: `http://site.com`

8. Click on the **Save Changes** button.

9. Back in your FTP client, delete all the files from your static site. If you want to back them up, copy them to your PC, but make sure they're all gone from your server to avoid any conflicts.

10. Now visit your site. You'll find that it uses your main domain name and not the subdirectory.

Summary

WordPress makes it easy for you to create a site that you can update and add to over time, letting you add posts, pages, and more without having to write code. In this chapter, you learned how to migrate your old static site into WordPress. You also learned how WordPress stores content, and how to install WordPress and import the content from your old site. You then configured your site, adding a theme, and menus, widgets, and plugins.

In the next chapter, you'll learn to create a social media site from scratch. So let's take a look!

2
Creating a Social Media Site

WordPress has a buddy that makes it much more powerful and lets you create social sites to engage with a community, allowing your community's members to talk to each other. It's called **BuddyPress**.

BuddyPress lets you create a powerful community site with a range of features you can turn on and off. There's a library of themes designed for BuddyPress, and you can also integrate it into the theme you're already running on your site.

In this chapter, you'll learn how to:

- Install BuddyPress
- Set up your theme
- Configure the BuddyPress settings
- Manage your site

So let's get started!

Introducing BuddyPress

BuddyPress is a plugin that you install as you would any other plugin, but it gives you much more functionality than some plugins. In this chapter, we'll work through all of the BuddyPress' features, configuring each of them in turn so that your site works as you need it to.

One of the great features of BuddyPress is that you can turn its features (or components) on and off according to your need; this means that you don't have to worry about anything that isn't relevant for your site. But in this chapter, we're going to look at all of it!

Uses of BuddyPress

BuddyPress has plenty of potential uses, but here are just a few:

- A network for a business or organization, letting colleagues communicate with each other
- A tool for coordinating a project or collaboration
- A community network for people interested in a specific topic
- A network to support a meetup group, letting its members keep in touch between meetings
- A network to promote a product or service and encourage customers and users to swap tips and talk about their experiences with the product

This is just the tip of the iceberg; BuddyPress is used for a wide range of applications by thousands of sites. In this chapter, we're going to build a networking site with all of the BuddyPress' components.

BuddyPress components

As I've already mentioned, BuddyPress isn't "all or nothing"; you can just activate those features which you need on your site. This reduces the code in your site and makes life simpler for you as the community manager.

BuddyPress features are referred to as components, which are as follows:

- **Extended Profiles**: This lets your users describe themselves in more detail than with a standard WordPress profile, and see each other's' profiles on your site's frontend
- **Account Settings**: This lets users modify their account settings from their profile page
- **Friend Connections**: This let users connect with each other
- **Private Messaging**: This let users send each other private messages
- **Activity Streams**: This displays streams of activity with threaded comments, favorites, and more
- **Notifications**: This notifies members of activity according to their preferences
- **User Groups**: This lets users create public or private groups with their own activity streams and member listings
- **Site Tracking**: This records new posts and comments from your site

As you work through this chapter, you'll learn more about each of these features, what they offer, and how to configure them.

Designing your social media site

Before you get started creating your site, it's worth taking some time to think about its design. This isn't just the visual design, but the **user interface** (**UI**) and components too. Think about the following:

Do you have an existing theme for your site that you want to use?

Is there a theme designed for BuddyPress (at `https://wordpress.org/themes/tags/buddypress`) that would work for your site?

What plugins are you already running on your site? Check whether they're compatible with BuddyPress; most well-written plugins should be, but any relating to membership or similar could cause a conflict.

What structure do you want your site to have? Will it include other elements that aren't part of BuddyPress, such as a blog and extra static pages?

What information do you want to include on each page using widgets? You might want to include a mix of BuddyPress-specific widgets and other widgets or just BuddyPress widgets.

What will be on your home page? This could be a static page, your main blog, or BuddyPress page.

Which BuddyPress components will you need to use? This will depend on your users' needs and the service you want your site to offer.

What BuddyPress components and pages will people be using the most? Make sure that these can be reached via one click from the home page.

How will people log in to your site? Will there be a separate login page or will you use a widget?

Spend some time thinking about how your site needs to work and look before you start, and you'll find that you're less likely to have to go back and redo things as you go along.

Installing BuddyPress

It's time to roll your sleeves up and install BuddyPress. This takes a matter of seconds and is no different from installing any plugin. Follow these steps:

1. In the WordPress admin, go to **Plugins** | **Add New**.
2. In the **Search Plugins** box, type `BuddyPress` and hit *Enter*.

3. Select the **BuddyPress** plugin and click on **Install Now**.

4. Once the plugin has installed, click on the **Activate** link on the page that appears to activate it.

5. Once BuddyPress has been activated on your site, you'll see the BuddyPress welcome screen:

Fig 2.1: The BuddyPress welcome screen

6. Click on the **Get Started** button to start setting BuddyPress up.

Configuring the BuddyPress settings

Now that you have BuddyPress installed, it's time to set it up.

Activating components

Before you can start working on your new BuddyPress site, you'll need to choose which components you want to activate.

This isn't the last chance you have to activate components; if you want to add (or delete) a component at a later date, you can do so.

If you haven't already clicked on the **Get Started** button or you're not in the BuddyPress welcome screen, go to **Settings | BuddyPress** to view the BuddyPress **Components** screen:

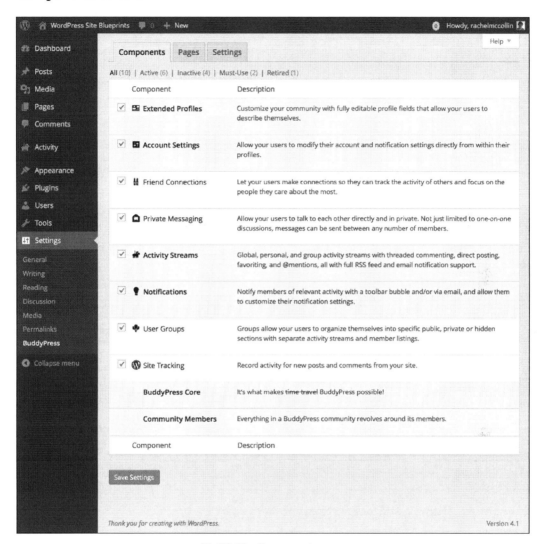

Fig 2.2: The Components screen

Tick the components you want to activate and click on the **Save Settings** button. I've ticked them all, I'm just greedy!

Now that you've got your components activated, the next step is to configure the pages BuddyPress will use.

Configuring pages

Click on the **Pages** tab to see the **Pages** settings screen:

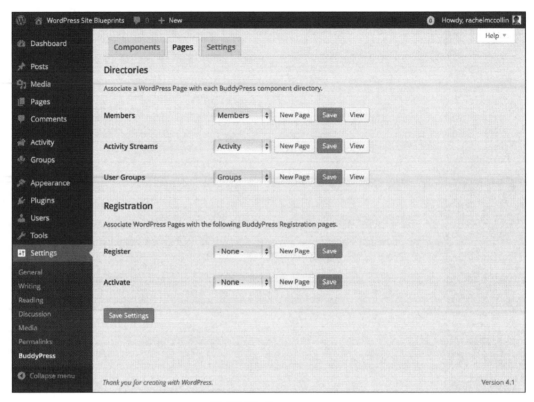

Fig 2.3: The Pages screen

As you can see, BuddyPress has created some empty pages in your site for use by the specific BuddyPress components. If you want to take a moment to check these, whizz on over to your **Pages** screen by clicking on **Pages** in your admin menu and then come back!

For each page, you can do one of these three things:

- Stick with the page that BuddyPress has created for you
- Select another page you've created on your site
- Use the **New Page** button to create a new page

We're going to stick with the pages BuddyPress has created in the **Directories** section, but we will need to create new pages for registration. Follow these steps:

1. Click on the **New Page** button for the **Register** page.

2. This will take you to the **Add New Page** screen.

3. Name your page `Registration` and click on the **Publish** button. Don't add any content to it.

4. Still in the page editing screen, click on **Add New**.

5. Name this new page `Activation` and click on the **Publish** button.

6. Return to the **Pages** settings screen by navigating to **Settings | BuddyPress** and clicking on the **Pages** tab.

7. For each of **Register** and **Activate**, select the relevant page from the drop-down list, as shown in the following screenshot:

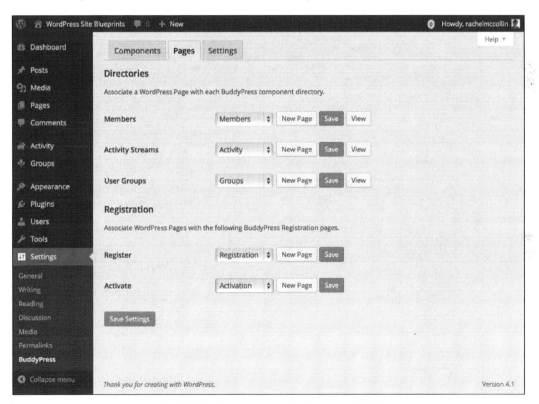

Fig 2.4: The Pages screen with all pages selected

8. Click on the **Save Settings** button.

Adding BuddyPress pages to your navigation menu

So that you can access and test your pages on the frontend of your site, you'll need to add them to your navigation menu. Follow these steps:

1. Open the **Menus** admin page by navigating to **Appearance | Menus** in the admin menu.

2. Click on the **create a new menu** link.

3. In the **Menu Name** box, type a name for your menu and click on the **Create Menu** button.

4. If you can see a **BuddyPress** metabox on the left with BuddyPress pages, great. If you can't see it, click on the **Screen Options** tab at the top of the screen. Under the **Show on screen** heading, check the **BuddyPress** checkbox. Click on the Screen Options tab again to hide this.

5. You'll now see an extra box, in the metabox on the left-hand side, called **BuddyPress**. Click on this to see a list of BuddyPress pages:

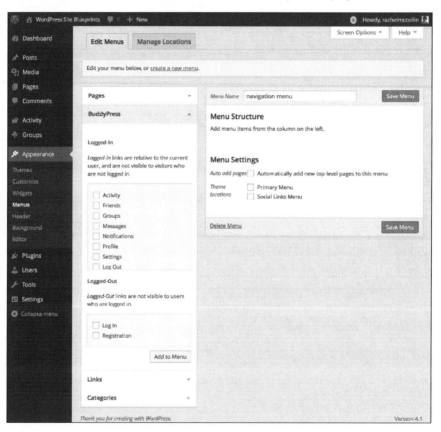

Fig 2.5: The Menus screen with BuddyPress pages visible

6. Tick each of the pages you want to add to the navigation menu and click on the **Add to Menu** button.

7. They will be added to your menu. Drag them up and down in your menu to get them in the right order.

8. Tick the checkbox for the theme location where you want your menu to appear. What this says will depend on your theme; I'm working with a fresh WordPress install, running the Twenty Fifteen theme right now, so I tick the **Primary Menu** box.

9. Click on the **Save Menu** button.

Your menu will now look something like this:

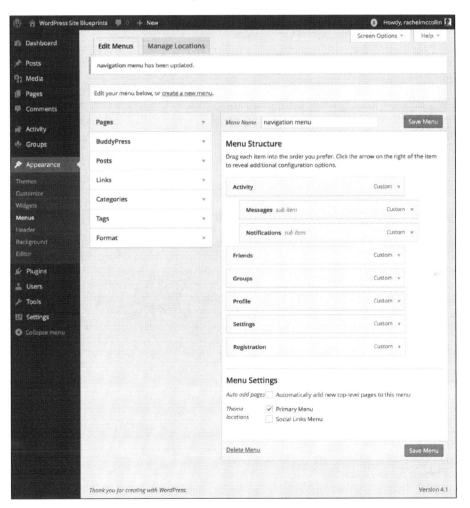

Fig 2.6: The Menus screen with a new menu created

The structure of your menu might be different from what I've used. Feel free to include the pages you need for your users and order them in the way you want.

Configuring home page settings

Now that you have your pages set up, the next thing is to tell WordPress which one of them will be the home page. Depending on the needs of your site and your users, you can have a static page, your main blog page, or a BuddyPress page. Here, we're going to set the BuddyPress **Activity** page as the home page:

1. Go to the **Reading Settings** screen by navigating to **Settings | Reading**.

2. Next to **Front page displays**, select the **A static page** radio button.

3. Next to **Front page**, select the **Activity** page from the drop-down list. Don't worry about the **Posts page** option for now.

4. Click on the **Save Changes** button to save what you've done:

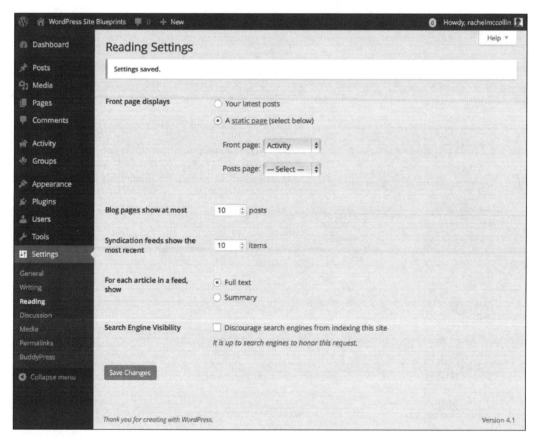

Fig 2.7: The Reading settings screen

Now that you have the **Activity** page set as the home page, it's a good idea to rename it in the navigation menu. Follow these steps:

1. Open the **Menus** screen again by navigating to **Appearance | Menus**.

2. Click on the **Custom Link** next to the **Activity** menu item. This will reveal a box with more options for that menu item.

3. Replace the text that says **Activity with Home**.

4. Click on **Save Menu**.

 Nothing you do on the **Menus** screen is autosaved by WordPress. You must click on the **Save Menu** button every time you make any changes.

The **Activity** page will now have been renamed as **Home** in your menu. Test it out by visiting the frontend of your site; when you click on the **Home** link, you'll go to the **Activity** page in your site.

Now that we have our BuddyPress pages created and added to the navigation, let's start configuring some other BuddyPress settings.

General settings

Let's start with the final tab in the BuddyPress settings screen—**Settings**.

1. Go to **Settings | BuddyPress** and click on the **Settings** tab. You will see a list of checkboxes related to components and features. These are:

   ◦ **Toolbar**: Tick this if you want people who aren't logged in to see the BuddyPress toolbar

   ◦ **Account Deletion**: Tick this if you want users to be able to delete their own accounts

   ◦ **Profile Syncing**: Tick this to sync user profiles between BuddyPress and WordPress

   ◦ **Profile Photo Uploads**: Tick this if you want users to be able to upload their own profile photo, overwriting the WordPress profile photo from Gravatar

   ◦ **Group Creation**: Select this if you want users other than the administrator to be able to create groups

- ○ **Blog & Forum Comments**: Tick this to allow commenting in the activity stream
- ○ **Activity auto-refresh**: Tick this to let the activity stream refresh without users refreshing their browser

2. Make sure they're all checked, as shown in the screenshot:

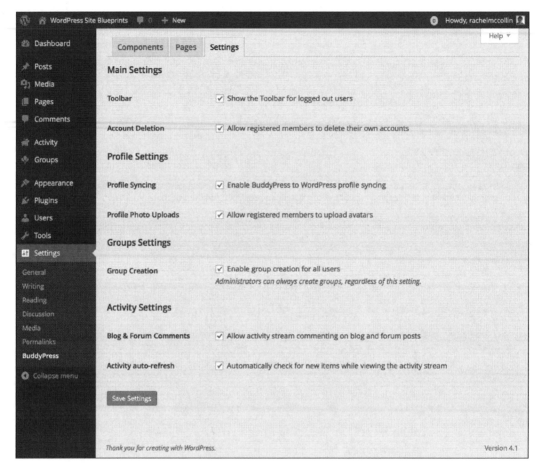

Fig 2.8: The BuddyPress general Settings tab with all options enabled

3. Click on **Save Settings** to save your changes.

You've now turned everything on to give your users the best possible experience from your site and BuddyPress.

Installing a theme

Having set up BuddyPress, you now need to install a theme that will work well with the design of your site. You may already have a theme you're using on your site, or one you're planning to install, which is great. If you're like me, you haven't identified a theme yet as your site is brand new.

If you've installed BuddyPress in a brand new WordPress site, your site will be running the default theme (currently Twenty Fifteen). Now I don't know about you, but I'd like something that's a little less generic and better suited to my site. So we have two options:

- Install a theme designed for BuddyPress
- Use BuddyPress with an existing theme

Let's take a look at each of these two options in turn.

Choosing a theme designed for BuddyPress

On the WordPress theme repository, you'll find themes that have been specifically designed for BuddyPress. If you visit `https://wordpress.org/themes/search/buddypress/`, you'll see all the themes that have been given the BuddyPress tag:

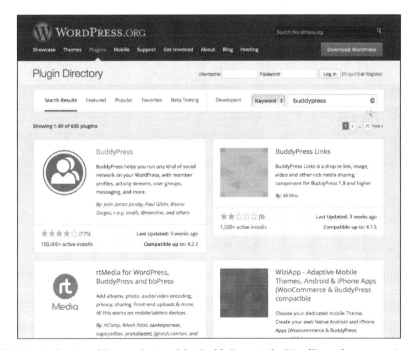

Fig 2.9: A selection of themes designed for BuddyPress in the WordPress theme repository

So, let's install a theme by performing these steps:

1.   Click on **Appearance** in the admin menu to see the screen for your themes.

2.   Click on the **Add New** button.

3.   In the **Add Themes** screen, click on the **Feature Filter** link.

4.   You'll be presented with a page listing of all the tags that you can use to identify the best theme for you. Scroll down and tick the **BuddyPress** checkbox, which is in the **Features** section. Depending on the needs of your site, you can also tick other tags such as colors or layout; let's tick the **Responsive Layout** and **Right Sidebar** boxes in the **Layout** section so that your site will work well on all the devices and have a sidebar where we can place some widgets.

5.   Scroll back up and click on the **Apply Filters** button.

You'll now be presented with a list of responsive themes with a right-hand sidebar designed for BuddyPress:

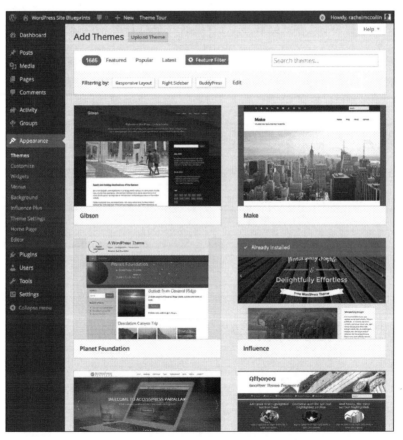

Fig 2.10: You have a lot of themes to choose from!

Feel free to experiment with some themes, installing and activating them and then checking how they look on your site.

For the site we're creating in this chapter, however, we're going to use the **Spacious theme**, which you can find at `https://wordpress.org/themes/spacious`. It's fully responsive (which means it will work well on mobile devices), has a right-hand sidebar, and also comes with plenty of theme options to let us customize our site.

To install Spacious, select it from the list of themes you're presented with (or do a new search with `Spacious` as the search term), then click on **Install** to install it, and eventually, click on the **Activate** link.

Let's take a look at how our site looks with the theme activated:

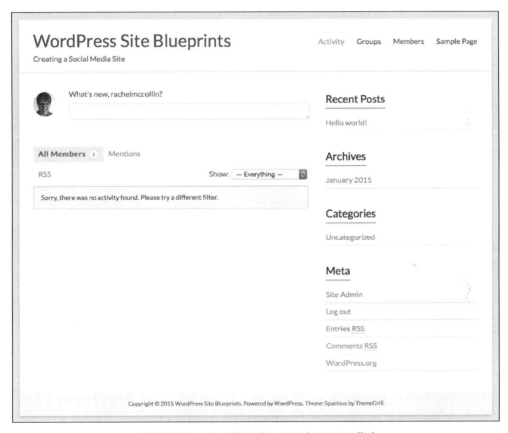

Fig 2.11: Our site with the Spacious theme installed

At the moment, it's using the default color (green) for links, and the default widgets have been added to the sidebar. We'll come to the widgets shortly, but first, we need to add our menu to the primary navigation in this theme.

Assigning our menu as the theme's primary menu

Whenever you install a new theme in WordPress, you need to revisit the **Menus** admin screen to make sure your menu is set to display in the space for a navigation menu contained in the theme's code. This is because each theme registers one or more navigation menus and you need to link those to the menu or menus you've created:

1. Go to **Appearance | Menus**. You'll see the menu we created earlier.

2. Click on the **Primary Menu** checkbox.

3. Click on the **Save Menu** button.

Your menu will now appear in the site header. Next, let's make some tweaks using the theme options screens.

Customizing the theme

This theme has some theme options screens, which you can use to customize the way your themes look. Perform these steps:

1. Go to **Appearance | Theme Options** to open the theme options screens.

   The tab, which will be open, lets you customize the header. Here, you can add a logo and specify whether that, your site title, or both, will be displayed. We'll stick with the site title as we don't have a logo for this site; this means that you don't have to make any changes on this tab.

2. Now click on the **Design** tab. This tab is provided by this theme, so you won't find it with all the themes, but it lets you make some customizations to the way your site looks. Select the following options:
   - **Site layout**: Wide layout with content width of 1218px
   - **Default layout**: Choose the option with a right-hand sidebar for the default layout and for pages and posts too.
   - **Blog Posts display type**: Keep this set to **Blog Image Large**.
   - **Primary color option**: Select a color from the color picker. I'm choosing a shade of blue.
   - **Color Skin**: Here, you can switch to a dark background, but I'll recommend sticking with the white one as it's easier for people to read.

3. Click on the **Save Options** button and take a look at your site now.

Here's how mine looks on an iPad in portrait orientation:

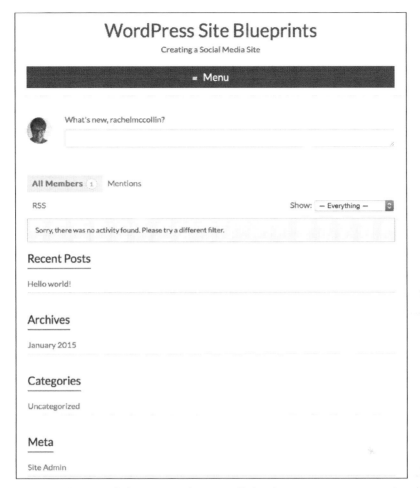

Fig 2.12: The site with the Spacious theme installed and some customizations made

You can see how the colors have changed and also how the layout adapts to the narrower screen width.

We're not going to make any more customizations using the **Themes** options screens, but you might want to take a look at them. They include:

- The option to upload and activate a favicon, via the **Additional** tab
- The option to activate and populate a slider with images and links to your content, via the **Slider** tab
- The option to add custom CSS in the **Design** tab to make further customizations to the design

So, now our theme is installed and set up. But what if you're already running a theme on your site and want to stick with that?

Using BuddyPress with an existing theme

Until BuddyPress version 1.7, using the plugin with your own theme was a little complicated. You had to create special theme template files, designed to handle the BuddyPress interface, and it meant that using BuddyPress with an existing theme wasn't always reliable. The styling of the BuddyPress screen components also meant that they often wouldn't fit into the layout provided by another theme.

The good news is that this has all changed. Since version 1.7, you don't have to use a theme designed for BuddyPress and add any extra files or (in most cases) tweak the styling to use BuddyPress with your existing theme.

You'll find that some themes work better than others with a social or community site, simply because their design and layout is more suited to the user interface you need, but in theory, you can use BuddyPress with any modern theme.

So, if you're not happy with the themes designed for BuddyPress, or you're already using a theme on your site, you can simply install BuddyPress, and you're good to go!

Adding widgets

OK, so now you've got BuddyPress set up, your theme installed, and things are looking good. Well done!

But you'll remember that earlier, in this chapter, we looked at the design of your site and the interface you want to give your users.

You've already done something toward helping people use your site by adding BuddyPress screens to your navigation menu, but you can do more. On a social site, it's helpful to have some content that users can see wherever they are on the site, such as the latest activity, a list of the groups they're in, and maybe, some help text.

To display content like this on every page, you can use widgets in your theme's sidebar and footer.

Let's start by taking a look at the widgets available to us.

Widgets provided by BuddyPress

To see the widgets that come bundled with BuddyPress, go to **Appearance |
Widgets** to see the **Widgets** admin screen:

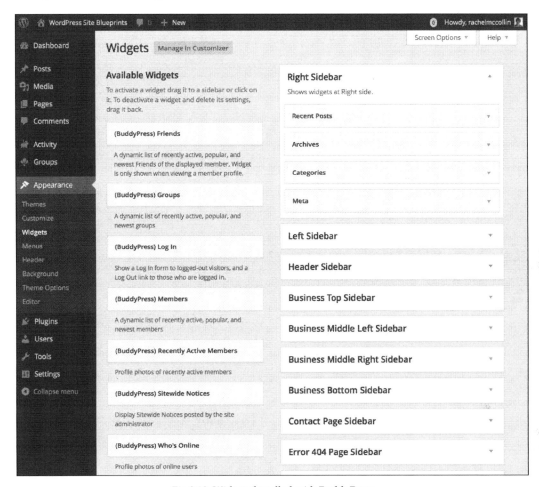

Fig 2.13: Widgets bundled with BuddyPress

The widgets you get are as follows:

- **(BuddyPress) Friends**: This is a list of the user's recently active, popular, and new friends
- **(BuddyPress) Groups**: This is a list of recently active and popular groups
- **(BuddyPress) Log In**: This is a login form (or a logout link if the user is logged in)
- **(BuddyPress) Members**: This is a list of recently active, popular, and new members
- **(BuddyPress) Recently Active Members**: This is a collection of the profile photos of the most recently active members
- **(BuddyPress) Sitewide Notices**: These are the notices you can post as the site administrator for users to see
- **(BuddyPress) Who's Online**: This is a collection of the profile photos of users who are online right now

Adding widgets to the site

Between them, these widgets give your users a wealth of information about their friends, groups, and activity. Let's add them to our sidebars by performing these steps:

1. If your site is a new WordPress installation, there will be some default widgets in the right-hand sidebar. Delete each of them by clicking on the down arrow, next to the widget title, then clicking on the **Delete** link.
2. Now, drag widgets into the positions where you want them. I'm using the following:
   - **Right Sidebar: (BuddyPress) Log In, (BuddyPress) Who's Online, (BuddyPress) Friends, (BuddyPress) Groups**
   - **Footer Sidebar One: (BuddyPress) Members**
   - **Footer Sidebar Two: (BuddyPress) Recently Active Members**
   - **Footer Sidebar Three: (BuddyPress) Sitewide Notices**
   - **Footer Sidebar Four: Meta (a native WordPress widget)**

Here's how the site frontend looks now:

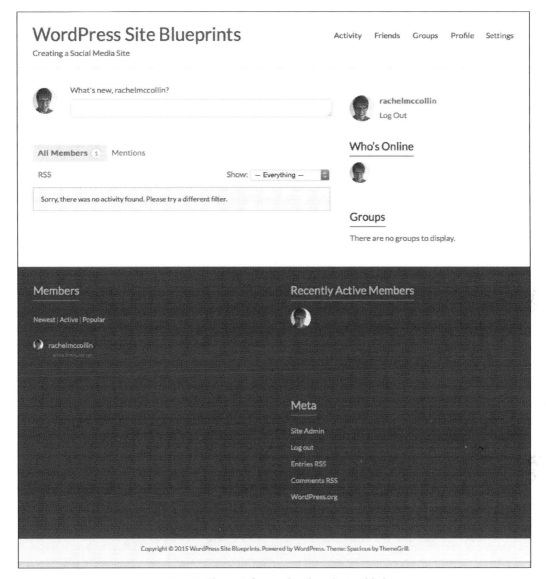

Fig 2.14: The site's frontend with widgets added

Note that the **Groups** widget is empty as we haven't created any groups yet, and there is a space in the footer where site-wide notices should be. But, we'll fix that next!

Adding a site-wide notice

You add site-wide notices on the frontend of your site using the **Messages** component. Follow these steps:

1. On the frontend of your site, go to the **Messages** page. In my site, it's under **Activity** in the navigation menu. This will display your messages:

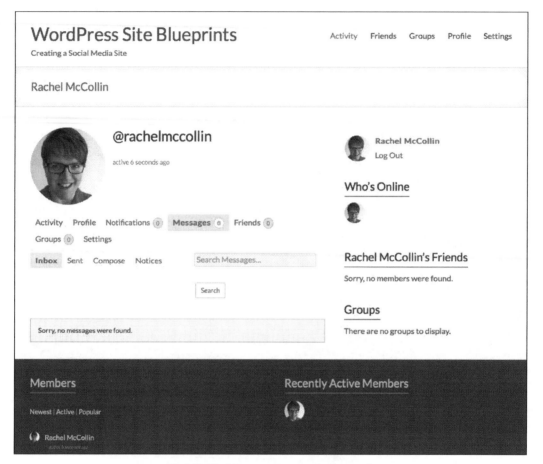

Fig 2.15: The Messages page on the frontend

2. Click on the **Compose** tab above the listed messages.
3. Tick the **This is a notice to all users** checkbox.
4. Fill in the **Subject** and **Message** fields.
5. Click on the **Send Message** button.

Now if you view the footer, you'll see your message:

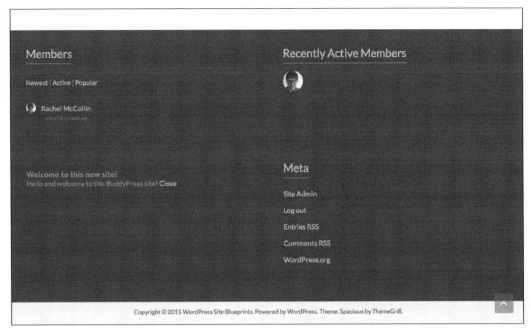

Fig 2.16: The footer with a site-wide message added

Testing your site

Now that you've got your site set up, you'll need to test it and see how it will work for your users. This means adding some test data so that there are some dummy users, groups, and connections.

Adding test data

The great news is that you don't have to manually add test data; there are plugins to do it for you. The BuddyPress Default Data plugin (`https://wordpress.org/plugins/bp-default-data/`) provides you with a set of data that you can use to test every part of your BuddyPress site. Follow these steps:

1. To install the plugin, go to **Plugins** | **Add New**.

2. Type `BuddyPress` Default Data in the **Search Plugins** box and hit *Enter*.

3. You will see a list of plugins that match the search terms. Find the BuddyPress Default Data plugin and click on the **Install Now** button for it. Click on **OK** when prompted to confirm that you want to install the plugin.

4. On the plugin installation screen, click on the **Activate** link.

5. Go to **Tools | BP Default Data** to see the plugin's screen.

6. Check the relevant boxes related to the user data you want to import to your site. Don't tick any of the boxes for groups yet; you have to do that after you've imported users.

7. Click on the **Import Selected Data** button.

8. Now repeat steps 6 and 7 for groups data; tick all of the boxes.

Your site will now have a load of BuddyPress data added to it. Take a look at your home page and it will look very different:

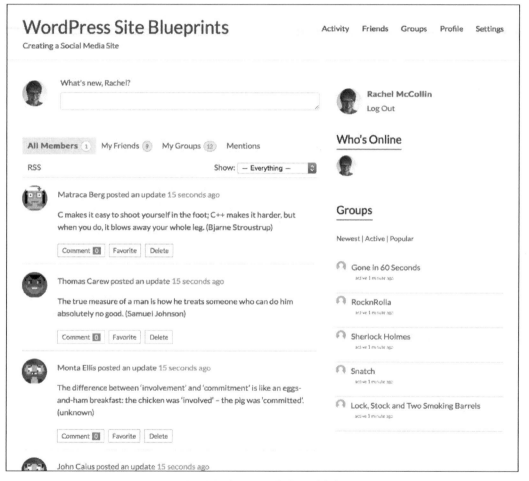

Fig 2.17: The site with data added

Now, let's use this data to test some of the BuddyPress pages and processes.

Testing the BuddyPress pages

Before launching your site, it makes sense to test out the pages you've added and the user interface you've created via navigation and widgets.

Spend some time working through each of the pages in your site, checking whether each of them is easy to find and whether the information in the sidebars and footer is useful and in the right place. You'll also need to check that everything is being displayed nicely in your theme; some themes with set width content areas might not fit all of the BuddyPress content in or might leave large spaces around it.

Here are the pages you'll need to check:

- **Activity**: Check whether everything is being displayed and that it fits in your theme's layout. Try posting an update.

- **Profile**: Check whether the table with profile information fits within your theme's layout on all screen widths. Try editing your profile and changing your photo. By default, BuddyPress will use the photo stored against users' e-mail addresses at `http://gravatar.com` if they have one, but this can be overridden if a user uploads a photo.

- **Notifications**: Check whether read and unread notifications are being displayed. Delete a notification or two and read some. Again, check whether they display on all screen sizes in your theme's content area.

- **Messages**: Check whether the tables for messages fit in your theme's content area. Test each of the tabs in the messages page—**Inbox**, **Sent**, **Compose**, and **Notices**.

- **Friends**: Check whether your friends' profile images and details are being displayed correctly in your theme and test whether cancelling a friendship works correctly, with the notification being displayed properly.

- **Groups**: Check your own **Groups** page as well as the pages for individual groups.

- **Profile pages**: Check out the profile pages of users who are and aren't your friends.

You don't need to check whether the BuddyPress components themselves work; instead, you should be checking that everything is being displayed correctly in your theme. The good news is that with the Spacious theme we're using, it all looks great!

The other benefit of doing this is that it will give you more familiarity with the BuddyPress interface, so if your users have questions for you, you can answer them easily.

Removing the test data

Now that you've familiarized yourself with your new BuddyPress site and tested it out with some dummy data, you'll want to think about launching it. But your users won't want to see all of that data you've used for testing. Don't worry; you can just delete it by following these steps:

1. Go to **Tools | BP Default Data**.
2. Click on the **Clear BuddyPress Data** button.
3. When promoted, click on **OK**.
4. Now check your site again. You'll find that all that's left is your own user activity.

Now, all you need to do is invite some users and fill the site up again with their activity!

Managing your BuddyPress site

The first step to managing your site is to get some users for it. If this is an internal site, for example, for a club or business, that won't be difficult as you have a readymade audience. If it's a public site, you'll need to use social media and other methods to make people aware of the site.

The most important factor that increases the chances of someone joining a social media or community site is the people already on it; if their friends are using it or there are other users who they find interesting, they're much more likely to join. So the more users you can get, the more you will gain!

Here are some tips to help you manage your site:

*   Spread the word as widely as you can. Use every opportunity to tell people about your site. Think about producing cards, stickers, or other fun items with the site's URL to give people so that they won't forget about it.

*   Make sure you're active on the site, and others will be too. Post engaging, interesting content that's relevant to the site's subject and purpose.

*   Keep an eye on who's joining your site and beware of spammers. Place a notice in your site telling people what the rules are and whether you will remove people who abuse those rules.

*   If members complain about comments or posts made by other members, investigate complaints with regard to the rules you've already defined, or that the community of members works together to define.

You can find out more about BuddyPress and how to get the most from it on the BuddyPress website at `https://buddypress.org`.

Summary

Now that you've worked through this chapter, you'll know that creating a great social media site for your group or community using BuddyPress isn't hard. You simply installed the plugin and made some amendments to the configuration to suit your site's needs.

In this chapter, you learned what BuddyPress is and how it works. You also learned how to install and configure BuddyPress. We also showed how to create pages for BuddyPress and how to add BuddyPress pages to your navigation menu. Finally, you also learned how to use BuddyPress with a suitable theme, how to add BuddyPress widgets to your theme's widget areas, and how to import test data to test out your BuddyPress site.

Now, all you need to do is grow your online community. Good luck!

Creating a Network of Sites

3

WordPress has a secret. Not only can you use it to create a single website for yourself or your clients, but you can also use one WordPress installation to create as many sites as you like, simply by activating **WordPress Multisite**.

In this chapter, you'll learn:

- What Multisite is
- When you might use it
- How to install Multisite
- How to create sites in your network
- How to let people create their own site on your network, with or without payment
- How to avoid splogs and spammy sites on your network

So, let's start by examining what Multisite is and how it can help you.

Introducing WordPress Multisite

So, what is Multisite? It's defined on the Codex as follows:

> *"A feature of WordPress 3.0 and later versions that allows multiple virtual sites to share a single WordPress installation."*

This means that by installing WordPress just once, you can run as many sites as you need. And what's even better is that these can all run different themes and plugins and have their own domain names too if you use a plugin to help with domain mapping.

We'll learn all about this as we work through this chapter.

Uses for Multisite

WordPress Multisite has three main uses:

- Creating a network of sites for use by one person or organization, for example, I use a Multisite installation at `http://rachelmccollin.com/` to host a network of demo sites, each of which supports a tutorial or book I've written. Organizations such as BBC America (`http://www.bbcamerica.com`) use Multisite to host a network of blogs.

- Hosting multiple client sites in one place. I use another Multisite network to host most of my clients' websites, meaning I only have to manage one WordPress installation and keep it up to date. Each site has its own theme and plugins, although many of the plugins are used by multiple sites, which means I only have to install the plugin once.

- Creating a network of sites, which will be owned and managed by other people. `http://wordpress.com/` is the largest example of this; it runs on one WordPress Multisite installation and hosts millions of sites, which are created by users. In this chapter, you'll learn how to set up a network like this.

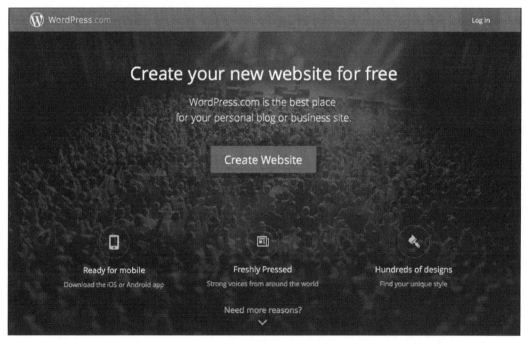

Fig 3.1: The site with data added

So now that you know what Multisite is and how you might use it, you need to learn how to install it.

Installing Multisite

You don't so much install Multisite as activate it: first you install WordPress in the normal way and then activate Multisite. But before doing so, you need to decide how your network will be structured—using subdomains or subdirectories.

Multisite structure – subdomain or subdirectory

You can use one of the two structures for URLs for the sites on your network, but you have to choose one before you start:

- Using subdomains means that each site will have a URL such as `http://site1.yoursite.com`. If you're planning to let people create their own site, you'll need to have wild card subdomains activated for your hosting. Find out more about wild card subdomains at `https://codex.wordpress.org/Configuring_Wildcard_Subdomains`.

- Using subdirectories means that each site will have a URL such as `http://yoursite.com/site1`. You can't choose this option on an established site that you're converting to a network as it may cause clashes with URLs already created in your site.

What you choose will be up to you. If you're going to be mapping domains onto your sites, it's irrelevant as no one will see the network's domain structure anyway.

For the network we'll be creating in this chapter, we'll use subdirectories. So let's do it!

Activating Multisite

Now it's time to activate Multisite by following these steps:

Install WordPress in the normal way. If you're not sure how to do this, *Chapter 1, Migrating a Static Site to WordPress*, shows you how. If you're working with a new site that you've already created, you can skip this step. Note that if you're working with a site that's more than a month old, you won't be able to use subdirectories for your sites.

1. Open your `wp-config.php` file, which you'll find in the folder where you installed WordPress. Find the line that reads:

   ```
   /* That's all, stop editing! Happy blogging. */
   ```

2. Right above this line, create a new line which reads:

   ```
   define( 'WP_ALLOW_MULTISITE', true );
   ```

3. Now save your file.

4. In the WordPress admin, go to **Tools | Network Setup**. You'll be prompted to choose subdomains or subdirectories for your installation; **choose subdirectories**.

5. Edit the title of your network and e-mail address of the network administrator (that is your e-mail address) when prompted or leave them as they are.

6. Click on the **Install** button.

7. You will be taken to the **Network Install** screen:

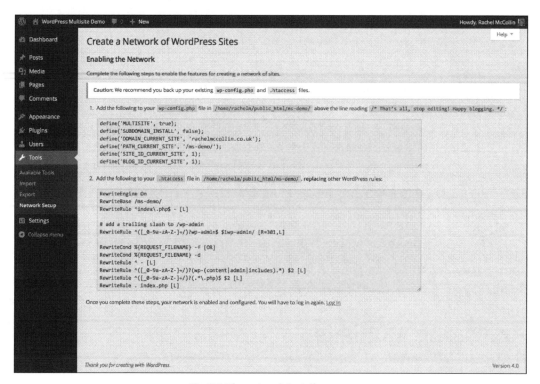

Fig 3.2: The network install screen

8. Open each of your `wp-config.php` and `.htaccess` files (both found in the folder where you installed WordPress) and edit them in line with the text provided on the screen. If you can't find `.htaccess` on your server, it may be because the hidden files aren't visible. Change the settings in your code editor if you're using one to access your files.

9. Save both files.

Well done! You've activated Multisite. You'll need to log out and log in to your site again, and when you do so, you'll see the dashboard. You'll notice that it now has a **My Sites** link in the admin bar:

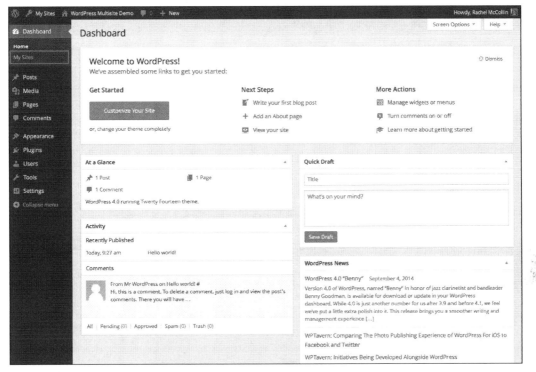

Fig 3.3: The Dashboard with Multisite enabled

Now that you've got Multisite enabled, you can start managing it.

The main site

Your network will already have one site activated, and that's the main site. This would have been your only site if you'd been working with a normal WordPress installation. If you're running a network that lets other people create their own sites, it's a good idea to use this site as your own site, with the content that will help people learn how to create their own site and encourage them to do so. You'll need to use a page in this site for the form, which lets users sign up, that you'll add later in this chapter.

Managing your network

Once you've got Multisite enabled, you'll need to manage your network of sites. This will consist of:

- Configuring the network settings
- Creating and managing sites
- Installing and activating themes
- Installing and deactivating plugins
- Installing updates

Let's look at each of these, starting with network settings.

Configuring network settings

Before you can allow people to start creating sites on your network, you'll need to configure your network settings. Follow these steps:

1. In the network admin screens, go to **Settings | Network Settings**.
2. Under **Registration Settings**, select the following options:
   - **Allow new registrations**: Tick the option that reads **Both sites and user accounts can be registered**
   - **Registration notification**: Tick this
   - **Add New Users**: Tick this
   - **Banned names**: WordPress adds some of these by default; add more if you would like to ban specific names, including inappropriate language or spammy links

3. Leave the other fields as they are. Your settings will now look similar to the following screenshot:

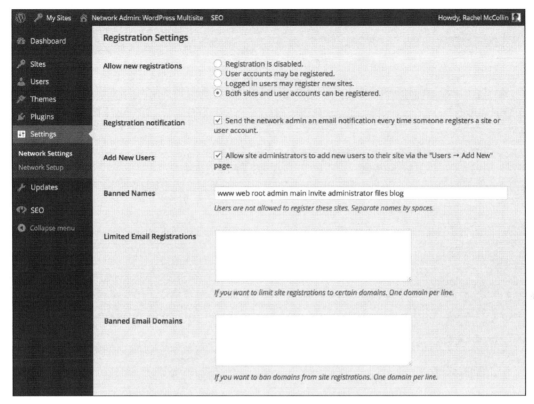

Fig 3.4: The Network Settings screen—Registration Settings

4. Now review the **New Site Settings** page. Edit each field if you want to, or leave them as they are. You might want to add some more detailed text for the first post, page, and comment on a new site to help users understand how these work, and how they can override or delete these default posts and pages. I've made some edits to the default settings which you can see in the next screenshot.

5. Review the **Upload Settings** options. You might want to increase or decrease the maximum uploads size, depending on your server configuration.

6. Make sure the language you're using in your network is selected under **Language Settings**.

7. Tick the **Plugins** box next to **Enable administration** menus in the **Menu Settings** section. This will allow site admins to view the plugins that are installed but not activated for the whole network and choose whether to activate them on their sites.

8. Finally, click on **Save Changes**.

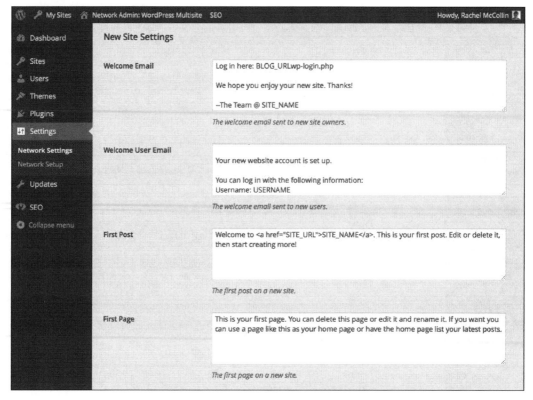

Fig 3.5: The Network Settings screen — New Site Settings

Creating sites

In this network, you'll let users create their own sites, but it's useful to know how to do it yourself. Let's create a demo site, which you can use to show people what they can do if they create a site in your network:

1. Go to the network admin screens by navigating to **My Sites | Network Admin** in the admin menu.

2. Go to **Sites | Add New**.

3. Type in the site address (that is the subdirectory), the site title, and the e-mail address of the site administrator, as shown in the following screenshot:

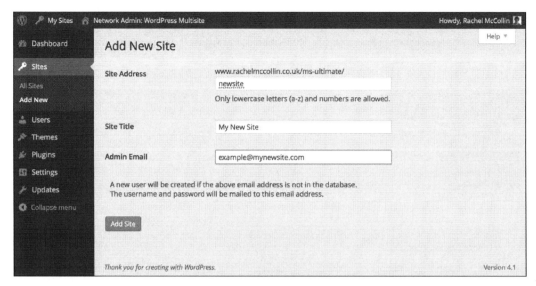

Fig 3.6: Adding a new site

4. Click on the **Add Site** button.

The new site will be created. If you've made yourself the site admin for the new site, it will show up in the **My Sites** menu in the admin bar. Click on its name to visit the site's dashboard. From here, you can manage the site just as you would manage a normal WordPress site, with a few differences.

Site administrator restrictions in a network

In many respects, administering a site in a Multisite network is the same as administering any WordPress site; you can create content, activate themes and plugins, and add users. However, there are a few things that site admins can't do:

- **Installing plugins**: For a site to have access to a plugin, it needs to be installed by the network administrator. As a network administrator, you can activate a plugin for the whole network or simply install it and leave it to site admins to activate the plugins they need.

- **Installing themes**: Only the network administrator can install themes and make them available for sites to use.

If you're not the site admin for this site, you can still access it from your network admin screens. Go to **Sites | All Sites** to view all of the sites on your network, as shown in the following screenshot:

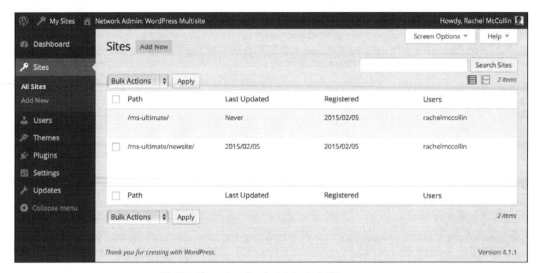

Fig 3.7: The network administrator's Sites screen

So, that's a new site created. Let's move on to installing themes for the sites in your network to use.

Installing themes

Only the network administrator can install themes and make them available for sites to use. You can do this in one of two ways: you can enable them for individual sites or you can network-enable them. For our network, we'll install some themes and network-enable them so that all of the site admins can choose from all of the installed themes.

Here's how you install a theme and network enable it:

1. In the network admin screens, go to **Themes | Add New** and install the theme in the same way as you would for a standard WordPress site.

2. On the **Installing Theme** screen that appears, click on the **Network Enable** link.

   Alternatively, to network-enable a theme you've already installed, click on **Themes** to go to the **Themes** screen and then click on the **Network Enable** link below a theme.

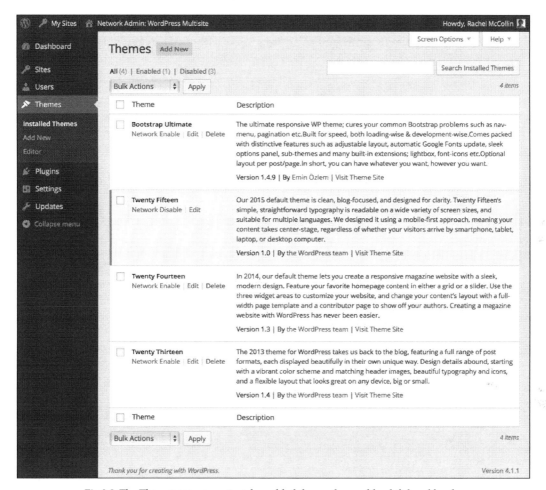

Fig 3.8: The Themes screen—network-enabled themes have a blue left-hand border

3. Find a few themes you like and repeat the preceding steps for all of them; five themes should do for now. Next, you can install some plugins.

Installing plugins

Again, only the network administrator can install plugins, but you can choose whether to activate them across your entire network or to allow the site admins to activate the ones they need. We'll use both approaches, starting with an SEO plugin, which we'll network-activate. Follow these steps:

1. In the network admin screens, go to **Plugins | Add New**. Find the plugin called **WordPress SEO** and install it as you would in a normal WordPress site.

2. In the **Installing Plugin** screen, click on the **Network Activate** link.

3. Now, if you go to the **Plugins** screen, you'll see your network-activated plugin highlighted with a blue left-hand border:

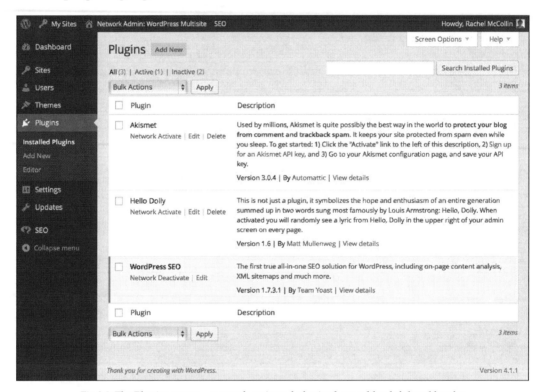

Fig 3.9: The Plugins screen—network-activated plugins have a blue left-hand border

4. Next, repeat the preceding steps for some more plugins, but don't network-activate them. Install an SEO plugin for your site owners to make use of SEO by Yoast (`https://wordpress.org/plugins/wordpress-seo/`).

5. Add any other plugins that you use a lot and think that people using your network would find them useful.

Now that you have your themes and plugins installed, it's time to set up the signup screen so that people can create a site on your network.

Allowing signups

So that people can register new sites on your network, you'll need to provide access to a signup page. WordPress automatically creates a signup page for you at `http://yoursite.com/wp-signup.php`. This isn't a very easy URL to remember, so we'll add it to your main site's menu to allow easy access:

1. Access your main site by clicking on **My Sites** and then its name by clicking on the **create a new menu** link.

2. Go to **Appearance | Menus**.

3. If you don't already have a menu, you'll need to create a new one. Type a name for your menu in the **Menu Name** field and click on the **Create Menu** button.

4. Add some of your site's content to your menu if you have it—the pages in your site and a link to your home page.

5. On the left-hand side, click on the **Links** option.

6. In the **URL** field, type `http://yoursite.com/wp-signup.php`, replacing `yoursite.com` with your site's domain name.

7. In the **Link Text** field, type `Sign Up`.

8. Click on the **Add to Menu** button.

9. Now, move the new link within your menu so that it's in the position where you want it.

10. If it isn't already, make sure the **Primary Menu** checkbox is ticked so that your menu is added to the right place in your theme.

11. Click on the **Save Menu** button.

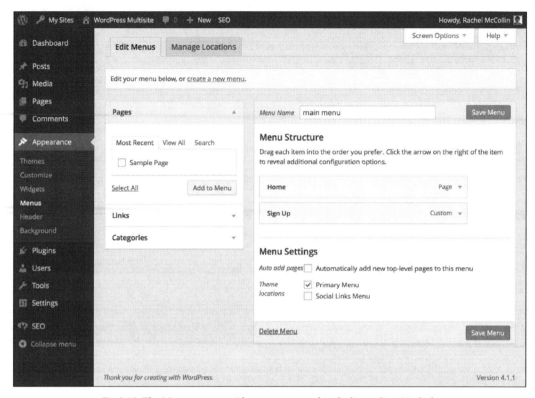

Fig 3.10: The Menus screen with a menu created including a Sign Up link

Now, you can test your signup page:

1. Log out of your site.
2. Go to the frontend of your main site and click on the **Sign Up** link.

You'll be presented with the signup screen. New users can use this to create new sites. Try it out!

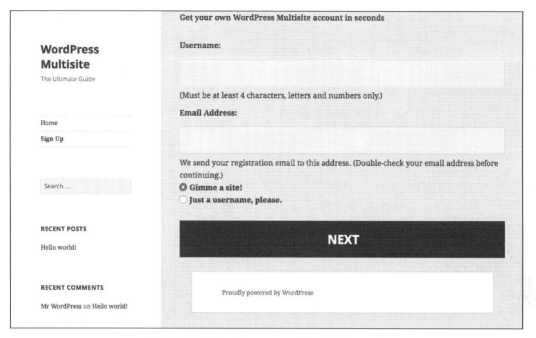

Fig 3.11: The Sign Up screen on the site's frontend

Letting users create their own sites is easy to do, but sometimes you'll want to prevent them from doing it, for example, if spammy sites are being created on your network. So, let's take a look at how to prevent this.

Preventing splogs

A splog is a spam blog or a spammy site created on your network. They're not created by people directly interacting with your **wp-signup** page, instead being created by an automated process that scans sites for forms. We're going to install a plugin that should prevent most of them. Follow these steps:

1. In your network admin screens, go to **Plugins | Add New**.
2. Find the **WangGuard** plugin and install it.
3. Now, go to the dashboard for your admin site by clicking on its name in the **My Sites** menu.
4. Click on **Plugins** to see the plugins screen.
5. Under the **WangGuard** plugin, click on the **Activate** link.

6. You will see the WangGuard welcome screen. Go to **WangGuard | Configuration** to set it up.

7. Click on the get one here link to get an API key so that you can use the plugin.

8. Fill out your details on the WangGuard site and click on the **Send** button.

9. WangGuard will send you an e-mail with a link to activate your account. When you receive this, click on the link.

10. Log in to your WangGuard account using the details you provided and copy your API key.

11. Paste the API key into the **Configuration** screen on your site.

12. Click on the **Update options** button:

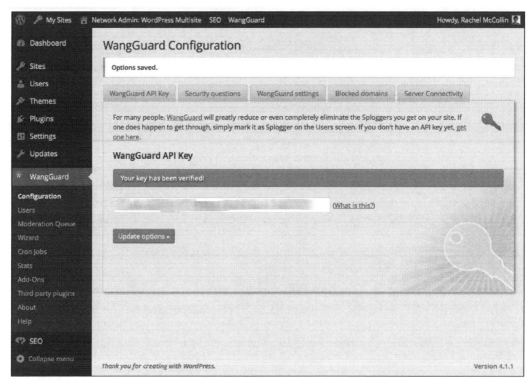

Fig 3.12: The WangGuard configuration screen with API key added

WanGuard will start blocking splogs, but it becomes more effective as it learns how your site is attacked, so it may be more effective over time.

Another option you might want to use to discourage spammy signups is to add a captcha element to your signup form. The WM Simple Captcha plugin (`https://wordpress.org/plugins/wm-simple-captcha/`) will add a captcha field to your registration form.

Adding payment for registration

So far, you've allowed anyone to create a new site on your network, and you've set up a plugin to prevent slogs. But what if you want to make money from your blog? It's possible to charge people to register a new site; let's set that up.

To set up payments, you'll need to complete a few steps:

1. Install the Paid Memberships Pro plugin and activate it on your main site.
2. Download and install the Paid Memberships Pro Network plugin.
3. Configure the Paid Memberships Pro membership settings.
4. Create a PayPal account if you don't already have one and upgrade your existing account to a free business account if you haven't already.
5. Set up **Instant Payment Notifications (IPN)** in PayPal.
6. Add your PayPal details to the Paid Memberships Pro configuration.
7. Create pages for managing memberships.

 You can add more features to the Paid memberships Pro plugin by installing one or more add-ons. Some of these are free, while others are premium. See `http://www.paidmembershipspro.com/add-ons/` for more information.

Installing and activating the paid memberships pro plugins

Let's start by installing and activating the plugin:

1. In the network admin screens, go to **Plugins** | **Add New**.
2. Find the **Paid Memberships Pro** plugin and install it. Don't network-activate it.
3. Go to the dashboard for your main site and then click on **Plugins** to go to the **Plugins** screen.
4. Find the **Paid Memberships Pro** plugin and click on the **Activate** link.

You will notice that a new menu item, **Memberships**, appears. This is where you'll configure the settings for the plugin.

Next, you'll need to manually install an add-on plugin that makes Paid Memberships Pro work with Multisite registration.

1. Go to `http://www.paidmembershipspro.com/add-ons/plugins-on-github/pmpro-network-multisite-membership/` to access the plugin.

2. Click on the **Sign Up Now to Access Download** button.

3. In your site's network admin screens, go to **Plugins | Add New**. Click on the **Upload Plugin** button.

4. Click on the **Choose File** button and find the ZIP file you just downloaded. Click on the **Install Now** button.

5. Go to the dashboard for your main site and navigate to the **Plugins** screen.

6. Find the **Paid memberships Pro Network Site Helper** plugin and click on the **Activate** link to activate it.

Configuring Memberships

Now that you have the plugins installed, you need to configure the settings. Start with membership levels:

1. Go to **Memberships | Membership Levels**. Click on the **Add New Level** button.

2. Enter the details for your membership level and click on **Save Level**.

You can see how I've configured membership for my site in the following screenshot:

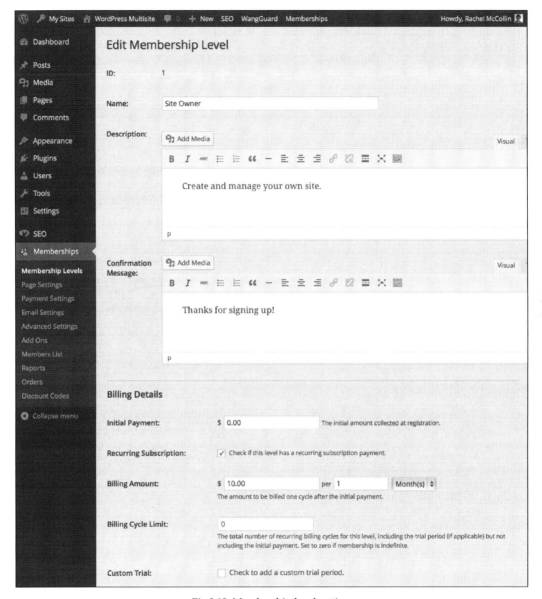

Fig 3.13: Membership level settings

Creating a PayPal account

The plugin uses PayPal to take payments from new users. If you don't already have an account, you'll need to set one up and if you do, you'll need to upgrade it to a free business account if you don't already have one. Follow these steps:

1. Go to `http://paypal.com` to sign in to PayPal or create a new account.

2. If you need to create a new account, follow the instructions provided. You'll need to wait for verification of your bank account before you can proceed.

3. If you don't have a business account, upgrade your personal account for free by following the instructions at `https://www.paypal.com/us/webapps/helpcenter/helphub/article/?solutionId=FAQ900`.

4. Once your PayPal account is set up, you'll need to link it to your site.

Configuring PayPal on your site

Adding PayPal to your site consists of two steps:

- Adding IPN
- Configuring the settings in the **Paid Memberships Pro** screens

Let's start with IPN by following these steps:

1. In your site admin, go to **Memberships | Payment Settings**.
2. Copy the IPN URL at the bottom of the screen.
3. Now, log in to your PayPal account and navigate to the IPN settings screen, which is in your account settings under **My selling preferences**.
4. Click on the **Update** link, which is next to **Instant Payment Notifications**.
5. Click on the **Edit settings** button.
6. In the **Notification URL** field, paste the URL you just copied.
7. Under IPN messages, click on the **Enabled** radio button.

8. Click on the **Save** button.

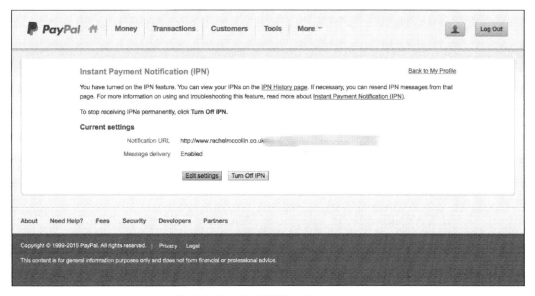

Fig 3.14: The PayPal IPN settings screen

Now that you have IPN set up, you need to add your PayPal details to your site. First, you'll need to request API access in PayPal:

1. In your selling preferences screen in PayPal, click on the **update** link next to **API Access**.

2. Click on the **Request API credentials** link and then tick the **Request API signature** button.

3. Click on **Agree and submit**. Keep this screen open so that you can copy the information provided.

4. Now, add your PayPal details in your site settings. Still in the **Payment Settings** screen in your site admin, complete the fields using the details provided with your PayPal account. You will find these in your profile page in PayPal:

   ○ **Payment Gateway**: Select **PayPal Website Payments Pro**

   ○ **Gateway Environment**: Select **Live/Production**

   ○ **Gateway account email**: Enter the e-mail account you use with PayPal

   ○ **API Username**: Copy this from the API information provided in PayPal

   ○ **API Password**: Copy this from the API information provided in PayPal

   ○ **API Signature**: Copy this from the API information provided in PayPal

5. Adjust the other settings as required or leave them as they are.

6. Click on the **Save Settings** button to save your changes.

Creating pages for membership and registration

The final step is to let the plugin generate pages for new registrations and account management. Follow these steps:

1. Go to **Memberships | Page Settings**.

2. Click on the **click here to let us generate them for you** link.

3. Click on the **Save Settings** button.

This will generate a set of pages to manage your site's memberships.

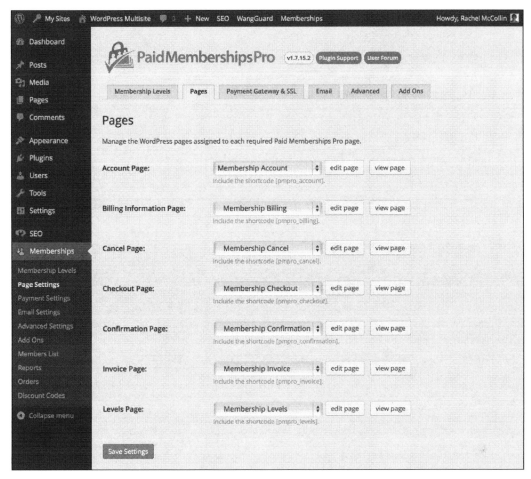

Fig 3.15: Generating membership pages

Next, you'll need to add the signup page generated by the plugin to your menu:

1. Go to **Appearance | Menus**.

2. Delete the link you created earlier to the **wp-signup** page by clicking on the downwards arrow next to it and then the **Remove** link.

3. In the **Pages** box on the left-hand side, tick the box next to the **Membership Account** page and click on the **Add to Menu** button.

4. Drag the page into the location in the menu where you want it to be.

5. Click on the downwards arrow next to its entry in the menu and edit the **Navigation Label** field so that it says **Sign Up**.

6. Click on **Save Menu** to save your changes.

7. Now check your registration page. Go to your site's frontend and click on the link to the account page.

You'll see a description of the membership level and cost:

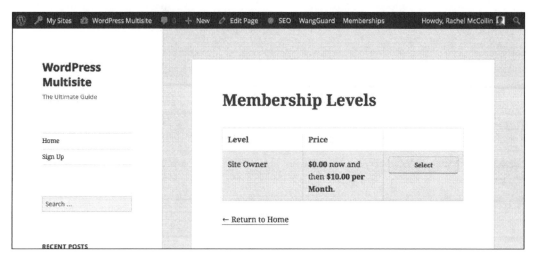

Fig 3.16: The Memberships page

If you click on the **Select** link, you'll be presented with a signup form:

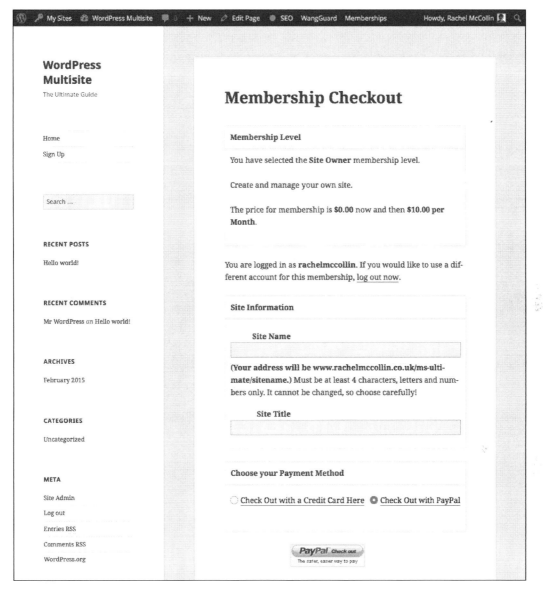

Fig 3.17: The Sign Up page

Here, users will be able to provide the details for their site and make payment, either via PayPal or using a credit card. Credit card payments are handled by PayPal. Once they've done this, they'll be returned to the site where they complete their site registration and can access their new site and its admin screens. You'll also receive an e-mail when someone pays for a new site.

Now that you have paid for registration setup, you can start making money from your network!

Managing your network

Once you've installed and configured your network and allowed user registration, you'll need to make sure that the network is constantly kept up to date, and manage the sites and users on it from time to time.

Managing sites

As a network administrator, you have access to all of the sites in your network and can manage them. There are four screens you can use to do this, and you can access them via the **Sites** menu link in your network screen screens:

- **Info**
- **Users**
- **Themes**
- **Settings**

Let's take a look at each of them.

The Info screen

The **Info** screen displays basic information on each site. This is where you would change the domain for the site, if needed, or update its status:

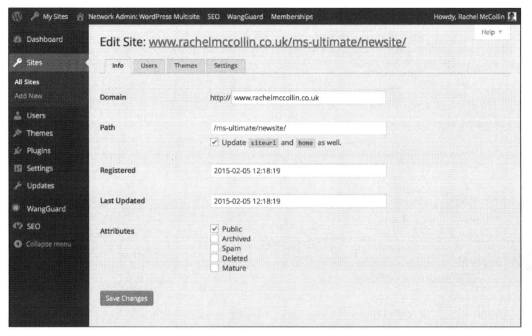

Fig 3.18: The Info page for a site

The Users screen

The **Users** screen lists all of the users for this site, who will also be the users on your network.

You can use this screen to remove users from a site or to add a user to a site if they've already been added to your network. You can also change user roles from here. Site admins can also add users from the **Users** section of their own admin as you would for a normal WordPress site.

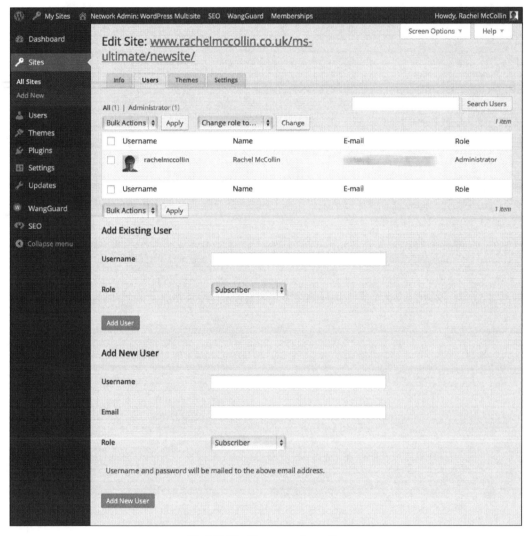

Fig 3.19: The Users page for a site

The Themes screen

You can use the **Themes** screen to activate a theme for just one site. This is useful if you're running a network of sites, which will each have a different theme, or if you don't want site admins to be able to activate themes that aren't relevant to their site. This might be useful if you're using Multisite to manage client sites, for example.

You can only activate or deactivate themes that haven't been network-activated here; this is why you won't always see all of your themes listed.

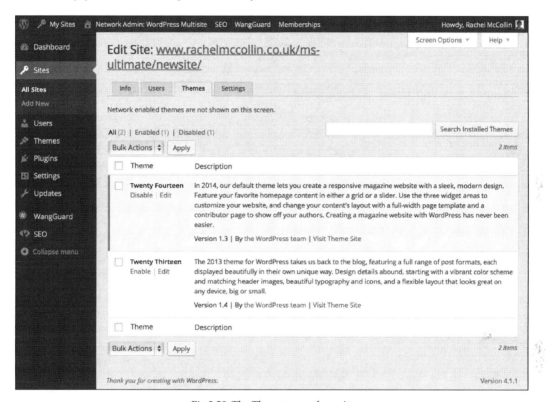

Fig 3.20: The Themes page for a site

The Settings screen

The **Settings** screen gives you access to all of the settings for each individual site, some of which site admins also have access to via the **Settings** section of their admin menu.

This includes everything in the site's options table in the database, including the site title, description, theme, and more. There are a lot of settings here; I would advise against changing any you're not familiar with!

Fig 3.21: The Settings page for a site

Keeping your network up to date

As well as managing individual sites, you'll also need to manage the network itself and make sure it's kept up to date. The elements you'll need to keep up to date are:

- WordPress
- Themes
- Plugins

Fortunately, WordPress will alert you to updates by adding a red circle next to the **Updates** link, joining the admin menu, with the number of updates available. The great thing is that you only need to update everything once, and all of your sites will be up to date. Make sure you take a backup of your site before updating though, in case of any problems. Even better, install a plugin that will automatically backup your site regularly, such as WordPress Backup to Dropbox (`https://wordpress.org/plugins/wordpress-backup-to-dropbox/`).

Managing users

As well as being able to manage users for each site, you also have a **Users** screen, which lets you manage all of the users in your network.

The **Users** screen works in the same way as it does for a standard WordPress site; it will list all of the users on your network and let you edit and delete them. This will include users that site admins have added to your site as well as users who've signed up for a site.

The one main difference is that the **Users** screen tells you which sites a user has access to. If you want to add a user to a site, you do so via the **Users** tab in the site settings.

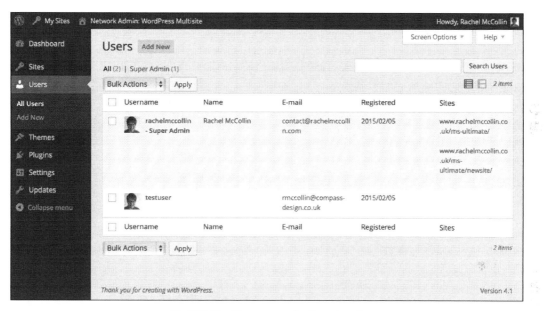

Fig 3.22: The Users screen for the network

Summary

WordPress Multisite is a powerful tool that can help you use WordPress much more efficiently. In this chapter, you learned about the users for Multisite and its benefits. You also learned how to install it, create sites on your network, and install and activate themes and plugins. You learned how to let users create their own sites, enable payment for this, and prevent splogs.

Managing your network on an ongoing basis is important and you learned about the screens in Multisite that help you do this. Now that you have a network in place, hopefully the sites on it will start to grow, but don't forget to look after it!

Creating an E-commerce Site

There are a variety of services out there that let you create an online store, but very few of them give you the flexibility of WordPress. Adding a store to WordPress is very easy; you simply install an e-commerce plugin such as **WooCommerce**, which is free and the most popular.

In this chapter, we'll do just that; we'll create a site and install the WooCommerce plugin along with the Storefront theme, which is designed specifically for use with WooCommerce. You'll add products to your store and configure settings such as payment and product settings.

So let's get started!

Planning your e-commerce site

Before getting started, it pays to spend some time planning your site. We're going to build a bookstore, which will also sell intangible products such as event tickets and downloads.

Planning product and department structure

While planning your store, think about:

- The products you're selling.
- How you're going to categorize them (that is, the departments in your store).
- Whether you'll use any tags (for example, I'll categorize my books by topic, but I'll have tags for e-books, paperbacks, and more).
- Whether your products are physical, virtual, and/or downloadable. I'll explain these in more detail as we work through the chapter.

Take some time to work through your products and identify how best to structure your store to encourage people to buy them.

Planning payment methods

You'll also need to identify how people will pay for your products. WooCommerce has a number of options for this, namely:

- BACS electronic payment
- Cheque
- Cash
- PayPal

In this chapter, we'll be using PayPal which is the most popular and convenient method to take payments. Customers don't have to have a PayPal account to make payments using PayPal; they can use their credit or debit card instead.

Planning shipping rates

Before you start, you'll need to identify how your products will be shipped to customers and what the cost will be. If your products are virtual, this won't be an issue, but for physical products, you'll need to identify how much the shipping will cost in your own country and how much it will cost for other countries you're selling to.

You'll also need to think about whether you'll use a flat rate for shipping each order or have a fee for each item, or maybe a combination of the two.

We'll cover this in more detail later in this chapter.

So now that you've worked out how you want your store to work, it's time to install WooCommerce!

Making your store secure with SSL

Before you start to create your store, you need to make sure your customers' details are secure. You do that by obtaining an SSL certificate for your site.

To set up SSL in WordPress, you'll need to carry out two steps:

1. Buy an SSL certificate for your domain.
2. Add SSL to your WordPress installation, either via a plugin or by editing your `wp-config.php` file.

Buying an SSL certificate

Most hosting providers or domain registrars will sell you an SSL certificate, which is normally the simplest way to go about it as they will complete the configuration with your domain name. Some hosting providers don't offer SSL certificates (notably, the cheaper ones), so it's worth checking when you're shopping around for hosting. Alternatively, if you want to do this yourself, you can buy one direct from an SSL certificate provider.

When you're buying your certificate, you'll have a few options to choose from:

- **Standard SSL Certificates**: These are sufficient for standard WordPress installations.

- **Extended Validation (EV) SSL Certificates**: These provide greater reassurance for website visitors as they turn the URL bar green and display the name of the organization providing the certificate.

- **Wildcard SSL Certificates**: If you're running a Multisite installation using subdomains (not subdirectories), you'll need one of these. These come either as standard or EV.

For this store, you'll need a standard certificate. Contact your hosting provider, and they'll sort that stage out for you.

Adding SSL to your WordPress installation

You have two options for adding SSL to your WordPress installation:

- **Add SSL manually**: To do this, follow the guide at `http://www.netorials.com/tutorials/how-to-set-up-ssl-in-wordpress/`. Note that you need to set up SSL for your whole site, not just the admin area.

- **Add SSL using a plugin**: The WordPress HTTPS plugin will help you add SSL to your site. Install it in the normal way and follow the instructions at `https://wordpress.org/plugins/wordpress-https/installation/`.

 When you visit the WordPress SSL's plugin's page, you'll see a warning that the plugin hasn't been updated for 2 years. This doesn't necessarily mean that it's out of date; it is just that it hasn't needed updating. I've used the plugin without any problems, but the most robust method, if you're comfortable doing it, is to install SSL manually.

Once you have SSL installed, it's time to start creating your shop.

Installing WooCommerce and the Storefront theme

To get your store up and running, you'll need to install the WooCommerce plugin and a compatible theme.

Installing WooCommerce

Let's start by installing the WooCommerce plugin:

1. Amid your WordPress, go to **Plugins** | **Add New**.
2. Search for **WooCommerce**.
3. When you find the plugin, click on the **Install Now** link.
4. Once the plugin has installed, click on the **Activate** link.

You'll now notice that a banner has appeared at the top of your **Plugins** screen, as shown in the following screenshot:

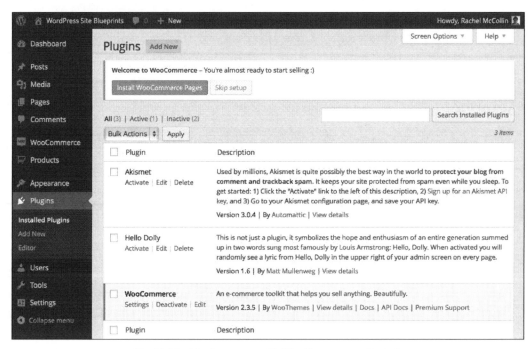

Fig 4.1: The Plugins screen with WooCommerce activated

You need to set up some WooCommerce pages to remove this banner and make your store ready to start selling. Follow these steps:

1. Click on the **Install WooCommerce Pages** button.

2. WooCommerce will create pages for your store, and you'll be taken to the WooCommerce welcome screen.

That's all you need to do! I guess you were expecting something more complicated.

Installing the Storefront theme

Now that we have WooCommerce installed, let's install a compatible theme. The Storefront theme has been produced by the team behind WooCommerce and is designed to work perfectly with it. Follow these steps:

1. In your admin menu, go to **Appearance | Themes**.

2. Click on the **Add New** button.

3. Type Storefront into the search box.

4. When you see the theme displayed, click on the **Install** button.

5. Once the theme has installed, click on the **Activate** link.

So, now we have WooCommerce installed and activated along with a compatible theme. Let's take a look at how the store looks now:

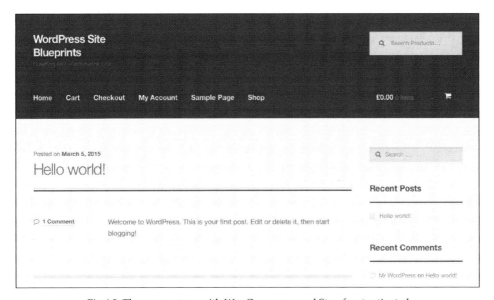

Fig 4.2: The empty store with WooCommerce and Storefront activated

Now that we have everything installed, let's configure the theme.

Customizing the Storefront theme

The theme has some customization options that you can use to make your store look how you want it to. Let's try them out.

1. In the admin menu, go to **Appearance | Customize**.

   You'll be presented with the theme customizer:

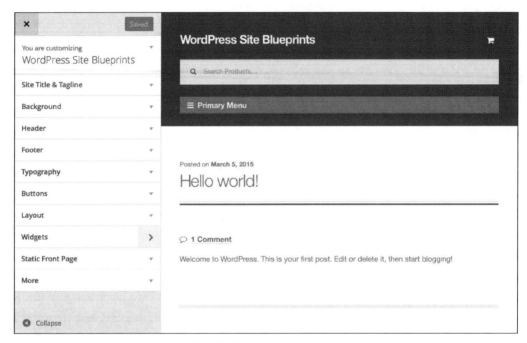

Fig 4.3: The theme customizer

2. First, let's customize a few of the colors in the theme. Follow these instructions if you want or play with the customization options to make the theme work how you want it to:

   ○ **Header**: Change the background color using the color picker

   ○ **Footer**: Use the color pickers to change the colors in your footer

   ○ **Typography**: Change the link colors to the same as your header background color

3. Next, let's change the layout. Click on the **Layout** link and select the option with the sidebar on the right. We'll use this sidebar to help people search the site.

4. Now click on the **Static Front Page** link. Instead of displaying blog posts, our home page is going to be the store's front page:

5. Click on the **A static page** radio button.

6. From the drop-down list under **Front Page**, select **Shop**.

7. Now click on the **Save & Publish** button.

Let's see how the store is looking now:

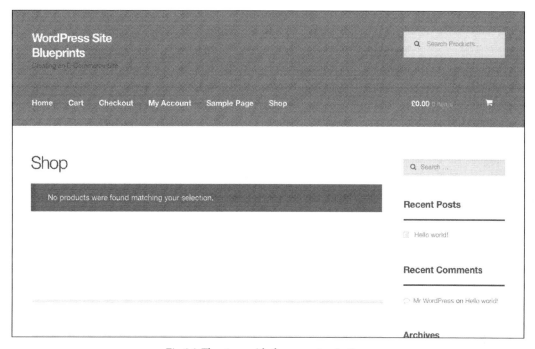

Fig 4.4: The store with theme customizations

The home page is now directing the user to the main shop, but there are no products displayed because we haven't added any yet; we'll fix that later in this chapter.

Adding store pages to your site's navigation

Before we move on to configuring WooCommerce setting, let's add some store pages to our navigation menu:

1. Go to **Appearance | Menus**.

2. If you don't already have a menu, create one by clicking on the **Create Menu** button and making it.

3. Drag the store pages you want to add to your navigation menu. Add the following:

    ○ **Shop**

    ○ **Cart**

    ○ **Checkout**

4. Now edit the link to the **Shop** page. Next to its entry in the navigation menu, click on the downwards arrow.

5. In the **Navigation Label** field, delete **Shop** and type Home.

6. Check the **Primary Menu** box to make your menu appear in the theme.

7. Click on **Save Menu** to save your changes.

Your store should now have the correct pages in the menu. We'll add some links to departments later on.

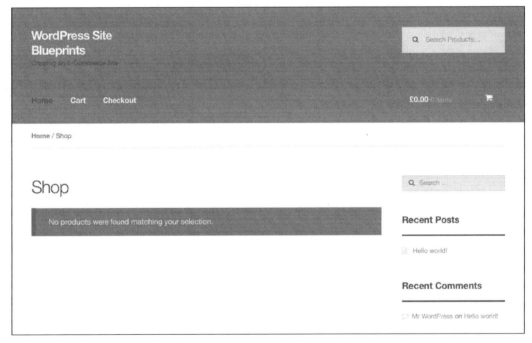

Fig 4.5: The store with shop pages added to the navigation menu

Adding widgets to the store theme

Now let's add some widgets to the sidebar. Perform these steps:

1. Go to **Appearance | Widgets**.

    You'll be presented with a range of widgets, including those provided by WooCommerce and the widget areas provided by the Storefront theme.

2. Add the following widgets to the widget areas:

    ○   **Sidebar**: **WooCommerce Layered Nav Filters, WooCommerce Layered Nav, WooCommerce Cart**

    ○   **Header**: **WooCommerce Product Search**

    ○   **Footer 1**: **WooCommerce Product Categories**

    ○   **Footer 2**: **WooCommerce Recently Viewed**

    ○   **Footer 3**: **WooCommerce Product Tags**

    ○   **Footer 4**: **WooCommerce Top Rated Products**

Now let's see how the site is looking:

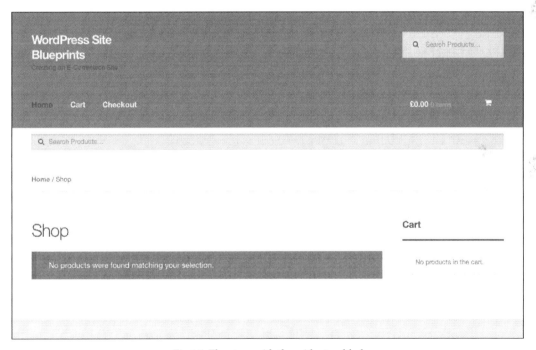

Fig 4.6: The store with the widgets added

It's still looking pretty empty because we haven't added any products or product categories yet, but that will change soon. Now let's start configuring the WooCommerce settings.

Configuring WooCommerce settings

WooCommerce has a number of settings screens you can use to configure your store. These come under the following headings:

- **General**
- **Products**
- **Tax**
- **Checkout**
- **Shipping**
- **Accounts**
- **Emails**

Let's start with the general settings.

Configuring the general settings

This is where you start configuring your store. Follow these steps:

1. In the admin menu, go to **WooCommerce | Settings**. If the **General Options** page doesn't appear, click on the **General** tab.
2. First, configure the general options:
   - **Base Location**: Select the country you're selling from. I've selected **United Kingdom (UK)**.
   - **Selling Location(s)**: We're just going to sell to the country we're selling from, so select **Sell to specific countries only**.
   - **Specific Countries**: Start typing the name of your county and WooCommerce will auto-complete its name. I've used **United Kingdom (UK)** as that's where I'm selling from. If you wanted to sell to more than one country you could add as many as you like here, for example, if you want to sell to all the countries in a continent.
   - **Default Customer Address**: Leave this as **Geolocate address**.
   - **Store Notice**: Leave these as they are by default.

3. Now configure the currency options:

   ° **Currency**: Select the currency you're using for your store. I'm using **Pounds Sterling (£)**.

   ° **Currency Position**: Select the positioning that's appropriate for your currency. I'm using **Left**.

   ° **Thousand separator**: Again, use the option that's appropriate for your currency. I'm using a comma here.

   ° **Decimal separator**: Choose the appropriate option for your currency; I'm using a period.

   ° **Number of decimals**: Select **2**.

4. Finally, click on the **Save changes** button.

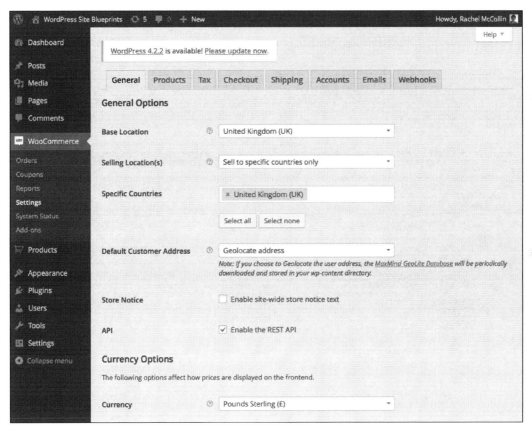

Fig 4.7: The general settings screen

Configuring the product settings

Now it's time to configure our product settings.

1. Click on the **Products** tab.

2. Leave the **General** product options as they are and click on the **Display** link to edit display options.

3. First, configure the product listings options:
    - **Shop Page**: Leave this as **Shop**
    - **Shop Page Display**: Select **Show products**
    - **Default Category Display**: Select **Show products**
    - **Default Product Sorting**: Select **Default sorting**
    - **Add to cart behaviour**: Uncheck the **Redirect to the cart page after successful addition option** and check the **Enable AJAX add to the cart buttons on archives** option

4. In the **Product Images** section, you can change the dimensions of your product images if you want. As the Storefront theme is designed to work with the default settings, we'll leave them as they are.

5. Click on the **Save changes** button.

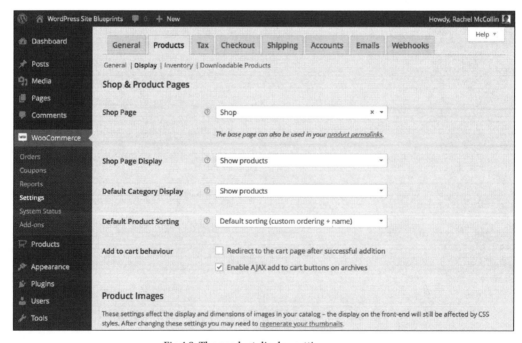

Fig 4.8: The product display settings screen

Still in the **Products** tab, let's move on to the **Inventory** screen.

1. Click on the **Inventory** link at the top of the screen.

2. Configure the **Inventory** options as follows:

     ○ **Manage Stock**: Check this box

     ○ **Hold Stock (minutes)**: Select **60**

     ○ **Notifications**: Check both boxes

     ○ **Notification Recipient**: Type in your e-mail address here

     ○ **Low Stock Threshold**: Select **2**

     ○ **Out of Stock Threshold**: Select **0**

     ○ **Out of Stock Visibility**: Uncheck this box

     ○ **Stock Display Format**: Select **Only show stock when low**

3. Now click on the **Save changes** button.

The changes I've made to my inventory settings mean that stock will be managed but the items that are out of stock won't be hidden for customers. They won't be able to buy these items now, but they'll know I sell them, so they may come back at a later date.

If your store only sells virtual products, you may not need to manage stock as it could be limitless, for example, if you're selling downloads. However, some virtual products, such as tickets, do need stock management.

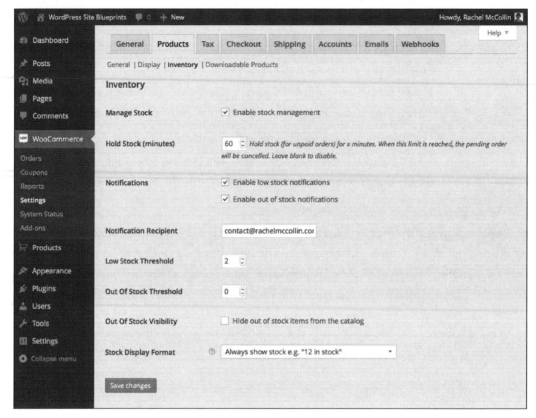

Fig 4.9: The inventory settings screen

Next, let's configure the downloadable products:

1. Click on the **Downloadable Products** link.
2. Next to **File Download Method**, select **Force Downloads**.
3. Uncheck the **Downloads require login** option.
4. Check the **Grant access to downloadable products after payment** option.

   These settings mean that your users will download products as soon as they've paid for them; they won't need to be logged in to your site to download what they've bought, and they'll be able to download products as soon as they've paid.

5.   Finally, click on the **Save changes** button to save what you've done.

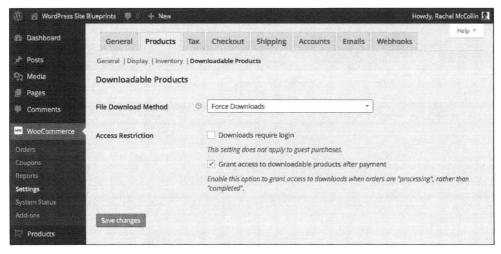

Fig 4.10: The downloadable products settings screen

Configuring the tax settings

Now that we have product settings configured, let's move on to tax settings.

1.   Click on the **Tax** tab in the **WooCommerce** Settings screen.

2.   Configure the settings as follows:

     ○ **Enable Taxes**: Check this box.

     ○ **Prices Entered With Tax**: Check the **No, I will enter prices exclusive of tax** option.

     ○ **Calculate Tax Based On**: Select **Customer shipping address**.

     ○ **Shipping Tax Class**: Select **Shipping tax class based on cart items**.

     ○ **Rounding**: Check this box.

     ○ **Additional Tax Classes**: Leave this as the default.

     ○ **Display Prices in the Shop**: Select **Including tax**.

     ○ **Display Prices During Cart and Checkout**: Select **Including tax**.

     ○ **Price Display Suffix**: Type `including taxes`, or if you're in UK, type including `VAT` (this is what I'm doing). You'll need to check what the tax requirements are for the products you're selling in your own country; in some countries, some products have sales tax applied, while others don't.

     ○ **Display Tax Totals**: Select **As a single total**.

3. Finally, click on the **Save changes** button to save your tax settings.

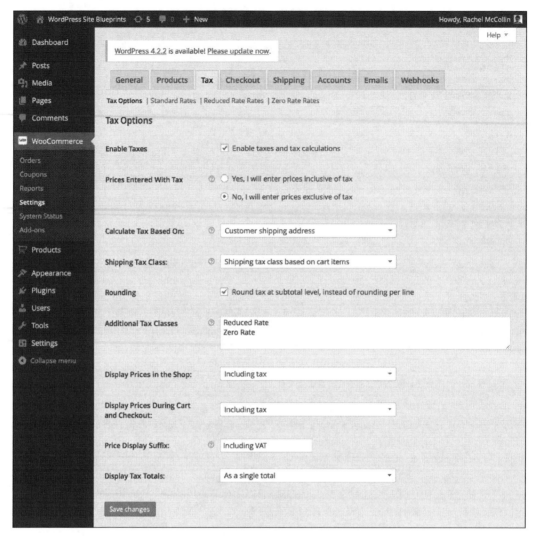

Fig 4.11: The Tax settings screen

The next step is to add your tax rate to the system. I'm going to be using a flat rate of percent as that's the rate in UK; you'll want to use a different rate if you're selling elsewhere. Follow these steps:

1. Still on the **Tax** settings screen, click on the **Standard Rates** link at the top of the screen.

2. Click on the **Insert row** button.

3. Type in your country or state code in the relevant column.

4. Type in the percentage tax rate in the **Rate** % column. I'm typing 20%.

5. If the tax has a name, type it in the **Tax Name** column. I'm typing VAT.

6. Click on the **Save changes** button to save your tax rate.

> You can add multiple tax rates, based on the different states and/ or countries you're selling to. To see a list of state and country codes, refer to http://creatingawebstore.com/woocommerce-country-codes-and-state-codes-list.html.

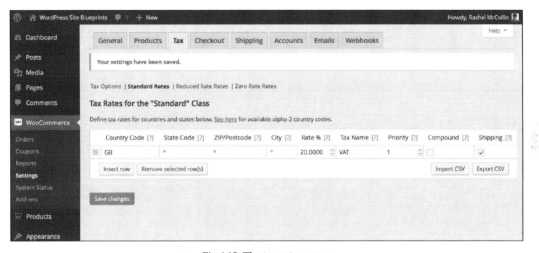

Fig 4.12: The tax rates screen

Some products in our store won't have any tax applied to them in the country I'm selling from, so we need to set up a zero rate of tax next:

1. Still in the tax settings screens, click on the **Zero Rate Rates** link at the top of the screen.

2. Add your country or state code again as before and then type **0** under the **Rate** % column.

3. Click on the **Save changes** button.

You now have the tax settings configured. Let's move on to the checkout settings.

> The tax rates that you'll need to set up will depend on the country and state you're selling from and to. I'm using UK tax rates; if you're trading elsewhere, you'll need to investigate your local tax rates.

Configuring the checkout settings

Now let's set up our checkout. This is where you add payment options.
Follow these steps:

1. Click on the **Checkout** tab.

2. Edit the **Checkout Process** options as follows:

    ◦   **Coupons**: Check this if you want your customers to be able to use coupons. I'm leaving it unchecked as I won't be using coupons.

    ◦   **Checkout**: Check **Enable guest checkout** and **Force secure checkout** (secure checkout is only available if your store has an SSL certificate).

3. Keep the options in the **Checkout Pages** section as the default. If you want you can add a **Terms and Conditions** page; you'll need to create a page in your site for this first and then select it.

4. Keep the settings under **Checkout Endpoints** as the default. These are the slugs for your checkout pages.

5. Under **Payment Gateways**, select **PayPal** as the default. We'll come to the payment options next.

6. Click on the **Save changes** button.

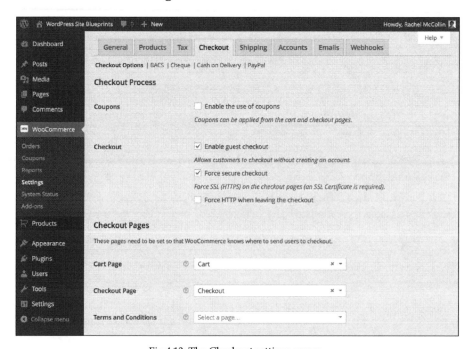

Fig 4.13: The Checkout settings screen

We're not using coupons in this store, but you might want to. They let your customer apply a coupon code at the checkout and get a discount. Use them for promotions and loyalty schemes.

Now we'll configure the payment gateways. First, let's disable the ones we don't want to use:

1. Still in the **Checkout** screens, click on the **BACS** link at the top of the screen.
2. Uncheck the **Enable Bank Transfer** box.
3. Click on the **Save Changes** button.
4. Click on the **Cheque** link at the top.
5. Uncheck the **Enable Cheque Payment** option.
6. Click on the **Save changes** button.
7. Repeat the preceding steps for the **Cash on Delivery** option, ensuring that it's unchecked (which it is, by default).

Now let's set PayPal up:

1. Click on the **PayPal** link at the top of the screen.
2. Edit the **PayPal** options as follows:
   ◦ Make sure the **Enable PayPal standard** option is checked
   ◦ Leave the **Title** and **Description** options as the default
   ◦ In the **PayPal Email** field, type in the e-mail address you use for PayPal

3. Scroll down and click on the **Save changes** button.

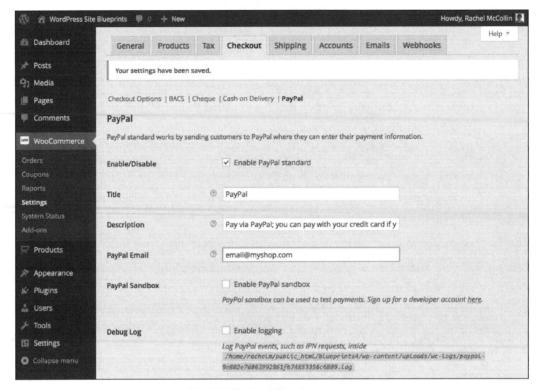

Fig 4.14: The PayPal settings screen

 For more information on how PayPal works with WooCommerce and the different PayPal options available to you, see `http://docs.woothemes.com/document/paypal-standard`. If you want to use PayPal in a testing environment before your store goes live, you can do this by checking the **Sandbox** option. Find out more about this at `https://clickwp.com/blog/woocommerce-paypal-sandbox/`.

So that's our checkout and payment settings configured. Now let's move on to shipping options.

Configuring the shipping settings

WooCommerce gives you a few options with regard to shipping. These options include:

- **Flat rate per order shipping**: With the same shipping for every order, no matter how many items
- **Per item shipping**: With the shipping cost directly related to the number of items bought
- **A combination of per order and per item shipping**: With a handling charge for the order and a per item shipping fee on top
- **Shipping classes**: Where different items have different shipping costs (for example, heavy items)
- **Shipping options**: Which customers can choose from, such as a choice of delivery speeds, with associated costs

Which ones you use in your store will depend on how you're going to be shipping products and what options you want to provide, as well as how much shipping is going to cost you. I'm going to use a shipping rate that comprises a handling fee and a per item charge, and not give customers the option to choose different shipping speeds.

Let's start with the **Shipping** options screen. Follow these steps:

1. In the WooCommerce **Settings** screen, click on the **Shipping** tab.
2. Leave the first few options as the default and scroll down to the **Shipping Methods** table.
3. Click on the **Flat Rate** link in the table.
4. Check the **Enable this shipping method** box.
5. In the **Method Title** field, change the text to `Shipping`.
6. In the **Availability** field, make sure **All Allowed Countries** is selected.
7. In **Tax Status**, change the status according to whether shipping is taxed in your country or state. It is where I live, so I'm selecting **Taxable**.
8. In the **Cost** field, type the cost of shipping.

9. Click on the **Save changes** button.

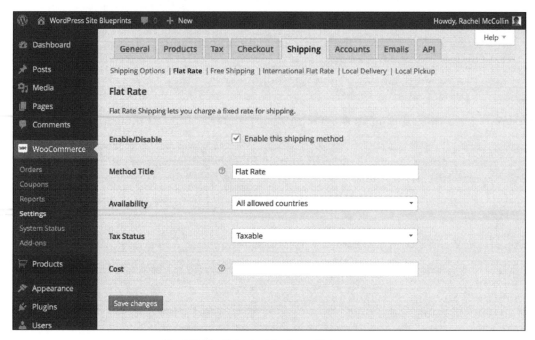

Fig 4.15: The flat rate shipping settings screen

Now, we need to disable other shipping options:

1. Click on the **Free Shipping** link.

2. Uncheck the **Enable Free Shipping** checkbox and click on **Save changes**.

3. Repeat the preceding steps for each of **International Delivery**, **Local Delivery**, and **Local Pickup**.

Now when you return to the **Shipping Options** screen and scroll down, you'll see that only one option is enabled:

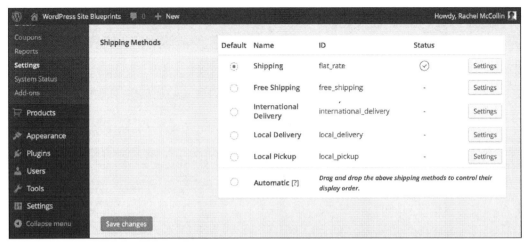

Fig 4.16: The shipping options screen with all the changes made

Configuring the account settings

You only need to make one small change to account settings. Follow these steps:

1. Click on the **Accounts** tab.

2. Under **Registration Options**, check the **Enable registration on the "My Account" page**.

3. Click on the **Save changes** button.

Configuring the e-mail settings

The e-mail settings screens let you configure the e-mails that are sent to you and to your customers when they make a purchase or create an account. Most of the default settings work just fine for our store, so we'll just make some changes to the general e-mail options:

1. In the WooCommerce **Settings** screen, click on the **Email** tab.

2. Edit the **"From" Name** and **"From" Email Address** fields if you want these to be different from your site title and admin e-mail address.

3. Change the **Base Colour** option using the color picker; use a color that you have already used when customizing the theme.

4. Click on **Save changes**.

So that's all of our WooCommerce settings done. Now it's time to add some products!

Adding products to your store

WooCommerce lets you add three main kinds of product to your store:

- **Physical products**, which are objects that you'll have to ship to your customers.
- **Virtual products**, which aren't tangible objects. These might include tickets for an event.
- **Downloadable products**, such as software.

You add all of these in similar ways using the same screen, but with some differences in what you need to add and configure.

For each product, you can add:

- A detailed product description
- A product summary or short description
- A product image
- A Stock Keeping Unit (SKU), which is a unique identifier
- Prices and shipping costs
- Inventory details to help you manage stock
- Product categories and tags
- Linked products, which will be displayed on the product's page in your store
- Attributes such as size
- Reviews

Now, let's work through the different types of product and add one or two of each.

Adding physical products

Let's start by adding a physical product:

1. Go to **Products | Add Product**.

    The product editing screen will be displayed. It should be familiar to you as it looks a lot like the screen you use to edit posts and pages in your site.

2. Type in the product's name in the **Product name** field and long description in the main editing pane.

3. Scroll down to the **Product Data** metabox.

4. Add the following:
   - **SKU**: Add a unique identifier for the product.
   - **Regular Price (£)**: Add the product's normal price.
   - **Sale Price (£)**: Leave this blank as we're not offering this item on sale right now.
   - **Tax Status**: If the item is taxable, select **Taxable**.
   - **Tax Class**: Select the correct tax class. My item is a book, which is zero rated in UK, so I'll select **Zero Rate**.

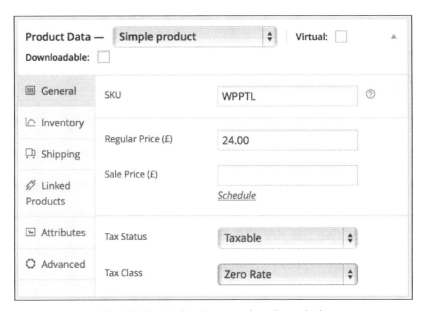

Fig 4.17: The Product Data metabox: General tab

5. Now click on the **Inventory** tab to the left of the **Product Data** metabox. Edit the options as follows:

- ° **Manage stock?**: Check this
- ° **Stock Qty**: Type in the number of items you have in stock
- ° Keep everything else as the default

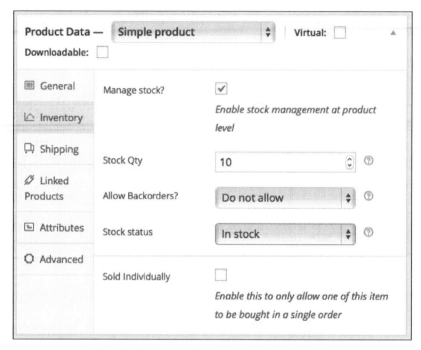

Fig 4.18: The Product Data metabox: Inventory tab

6. Next, click on the **Advanced** tab and check the **Enable reviews** box.

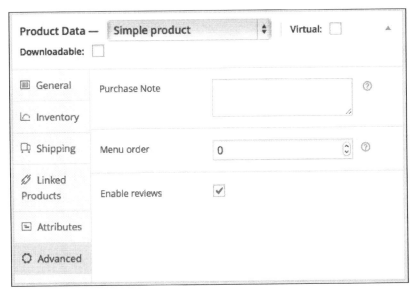

Fig 4.19: The Product Data metabox: Advanced tab

7. Scroll down and add a short description of the product in the **Product Short Description** metabox. This will display at the top of the product's page.

8. Next, move back up to the **Product Categories** metabox on the right-hand side of the editing screen. Your store doesn't have any product categories yet, but you can add one or more here. I'm going to add one called **Books**.

9. Now add as many product tags as you'd like. My book is an advanced WordPress development book, so I'm going to add three tags: **Advanced**, **Web Development**, and **WordPress**.

10. Upload a featured image for your product. This is the main product image that will display on your product page and on the main shop page.

11. If you have more images, add images to the **Product Gallery** metabox.

12. Finally, click on the **Publish** button.

WordPress will save your product for you:

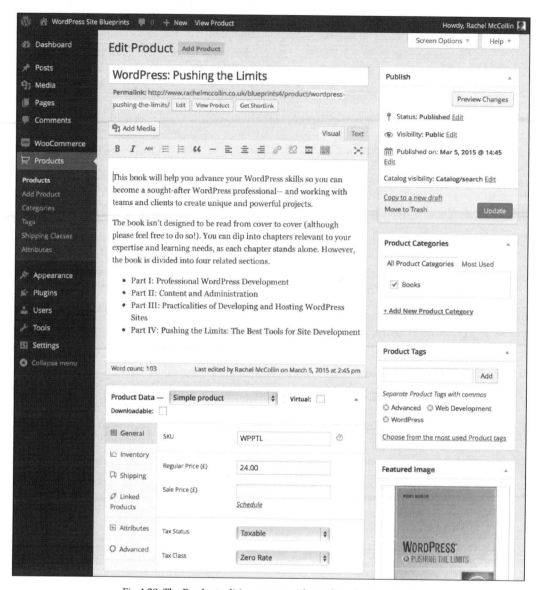

Fig 4.20: The Product editing screen with product details added

Click on the **View Product** link in the admin bar to see your product. Here's mine:

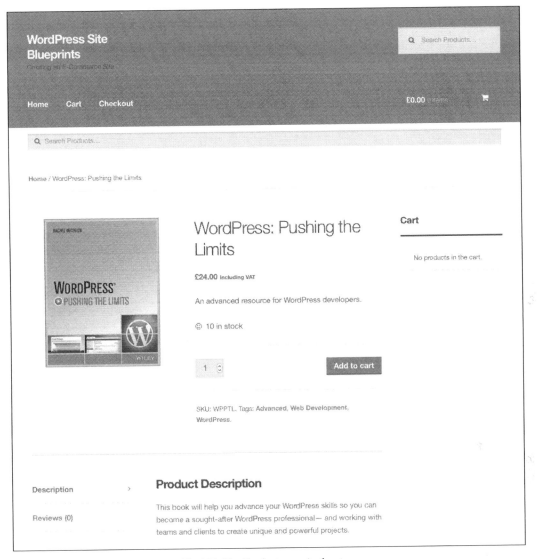

Fig 4.21: The Product page in the store

Now let's add another product, which will be a linked product to the first one. Linked products are used to display extra products on a single product page which shoppers might want to buy as well as the first product. Follow these steps:

1. In the admin menu, go to **Products** | **Add Product**.

2. Add your second product in the same way as you did the first. Don't click on the **Publish** button yet.

3. In the **Product Data** metabox, click on the **Linked Products** tab.

4. In the **Cross-Sells** field, start typing the name of the first product you added. WordPress will find the product for you and autocomplete the field.

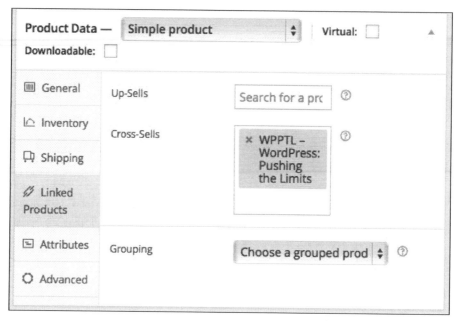

Fig 4.22: The Product Data metabox: the Linked Products tab

5. Click on the **Publish** button.

Let's take a look at this second product in the store. If you open its page and scroll down, you'll see a **Related Products** section:

Fig 4.23: The Related Products section of the Product page

Now that we've added a couple of physical products, let's move on to adding a virtual product.

Adding virtual products

I'm going to add a virtual product, which will be a ticket to an online event my bookstore is hosting. Follow these steps:

1. In the admin menu, go to **Products** | **Add Product**.

2. Add the details of your product, categories, tags, and a featured image in the same way as you did for your physical products. I'm adding a new category called **Events**.

3. In the **Product Data** metabox, tick the **Virtual** checkbox.

4. The **Product Data** metabox will change and the **Shipping** tab will disappear as you can't ship virtual products.

5. Now, complete the tabs in the **Product Data** metabox in the same way as you did for your other products.

6. Click on the **Publish** button.

Well done, you've added a virtual product! Here's how mine looks in my store:

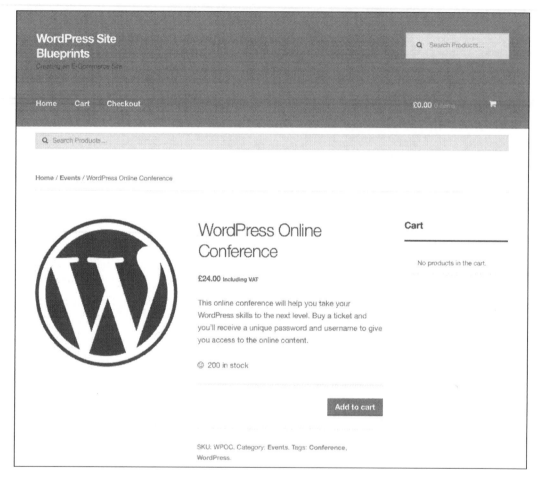

Fig 4.24: The new virtual product in my store

Adding downloadable products

As well as virtual products, you can also use WooCommerce to see products that people can download, such as PDF guides or software. Let's add a downloadable product now:

1. In the admin menu, go to **Products | Add Product**.

2. Add your product's details as you would for any other product, including descriptions, categories, tags, and a featured image. I'm adding a new category called **Downloads**.

3. In the **Product Data** metabox, tick the **Virtual** and **Downloadable** checkboxes. The reason you have to check both is because sometimes a product might be physical and downloadable, for example, software that people could have sent to them or downloaded.

4. The **General** tab will change to include a **Downloadable Files** section.

5. Add the **SKU** and **Price** for the product as normal.

6. In the **Downloadable Files** section, click on the **Add File** button.

7. You can either add a link to a file that you have already hosted elsewhere or click on the **Choose file** button to upload it using the Media Uploader. I'm going to upload my file, so I'll click on the **Choose file** button.

8. In the Media Uploader, upload your file and click on the **Insert file URL** button.

9. The URL will be added to the **File URL** field.

10. Now type in the name for your file in the **Name** field.

11. In the **Download Limit** field, type the number of downloads each customer can make once they've paid for the product. I'm typing 1.

12. If you want the download link to expire after a number of days, type the number of days in the **Download Expiry** field. I'm setting this at **7**.

13. Next to **Download Type**, select **Standard Product**.

Your metabox will look something similar to this:

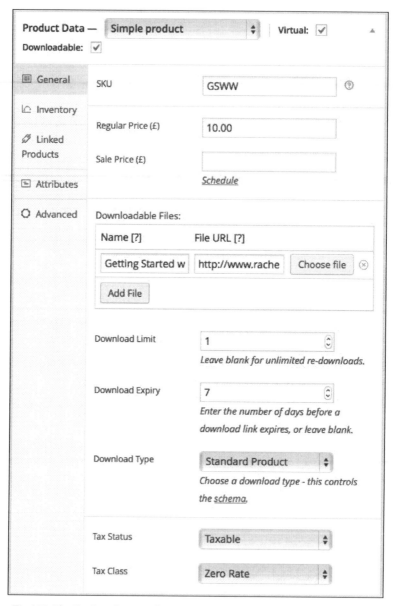

Fig 4.25: The Product data metabox: the General tab for downloadable products

14. Now complete the other tabs in the **Product Data** metabox as you would for any product. I'm not using stock management for my product as the number of downloads need not be limited.

15. Hit the **Publish** button to save your new product.

Here's how my product looks in my store:

Fig 4.26: The new downloadable product in my store

So that's all a downloadable product added. When people buy the downloadable product, they'll be given access to a secure link from where they can make the download.

Updating the navigation

Now that we have some product categories, let's add them to the main navigation menu:

1. In the admin menu, go to **Appearance | Menus**.

2. If your product categories aren't visible on the left-hand side, click on the **Screen Options** tab at the very top of the screen.

3. Tick the **Product Categories** checkbox and close the **Screen Options** tab.

4. Now expand the **Product Categories** box on the left-hand side and select each of your product categories.

5. Click on the **Add to Menu** button.

6. Move the product categories in your menu so that they're where you want them to be. Here's mine:

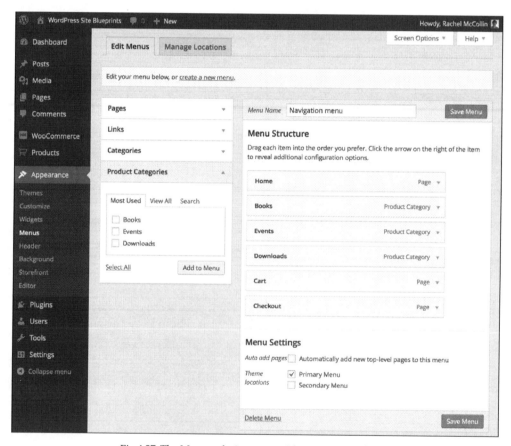

Fig 4.27: The Menus admin screen with my menu updated

7. Click on the **Save Menu** button.

Now my site includes the main product categories in the menu:

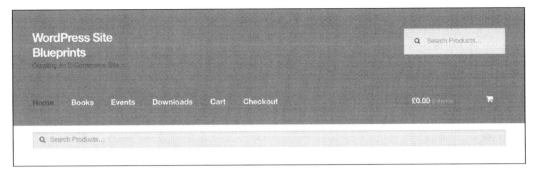

Fig 4.28: The updated menu in my site

Managing your store

Now that you have some products in your store, you'll need to spend time managing it on an ongoing basis. This will include:

- Adding new products
- Running sales to promote products
- Managing orders

Let's have a look at how you manage orders.

Managing orders

When you receive a new order and it's successfully paid for, you'll receive an e-mail notification. You'll then need to manage that order and ship the product. Follow these steps:

1. In the admin menu, go to **WooCommerce | Orders**.

    You'll see your new order or orders displayed:

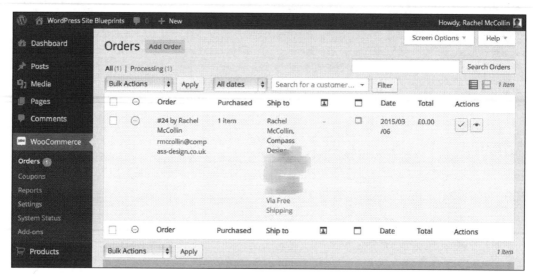

Fig 4.29: The Orders screen

The orders you haven't processed yet have a green circle next to them to show that they're being processed.

2. Click on the order number to see its screen:

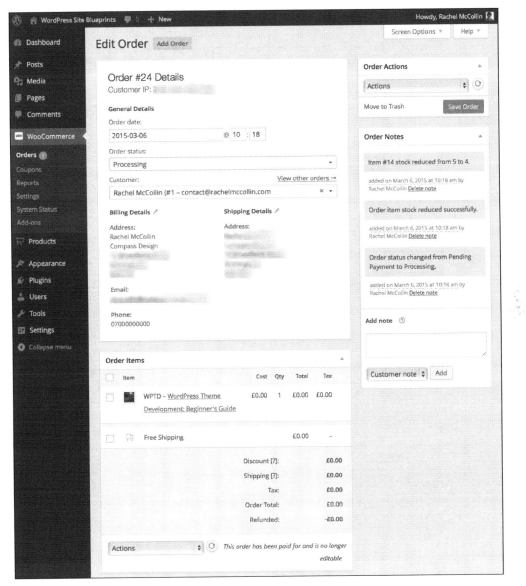

Fig 4.30: The individual order management screen

3. Once you've processed the order and shipped the item, change the **Order status** value. Select **Completed** from the drop-down box.

4. Click on the **Save Order** button.

When you return to the **Orders** screen, you'll see that the processing symbol has been replaced by a tick to show that the order is complete.

Note that you won't need to manage orders for virtual or downloadable products like this as they will automatically be delivered to customers. You can still see them in the **Orders** screen though.

Summary

Well done, you now have a functioning online store using WordPress, the WooCommerce plugin, and Storefront theme. You can take your store further by using one or more of the extensions that are available for WooCommerce; find out more at http://www.woothemes.com/product-category/woocommerce-extensions/.

In this chapter, you learned how to create your store and add physical, virtual, and downloadable products. You also learned how to customize your theme, configure WooCommerce settings, and manage orders.

In the next chapter, we'll learn how to set up a video streaming site. Meanwhile, good luck with your store!

5
Creating a Video Streaming Site

Sharing content, entertainment, and ideas via video rather than text is becoming more of a phenomenon. Vlogging (that is, video blogging) is fast becoming as popular as regular blogging, and can be big business; some of the most popular YouTubers (as YouTube broadcasters are known) make millions of dollars a year, have a fan base in the millions, and are being offered their own TV programs.

If you want to create and share videos, the most popular platform to use is YouTube, but you can also use WordPress in conjunction with YouTube to create your own video steaming site. A lot of successful YouTubers have started creating their own site to stream their videos, connect with their fans, and even sell merchandise, all from one place. WordPress gives you plenty of tools to do this.

In this chapter, you'll learn how to stream video from YouTube to your own video sharing site, meaning that you can add more than just the videos to your site and have complete control over how your videos are shown. We'll create a channel on YouTube and then set up a WordPress site with a theme and plugin to help us stream video from that channel.

Planning your video streaming site

The first step is to plan how you want to use your video site. Ask yourself a few questions:

- Will I be streaming all my video from YouTube?
- Will I be uploading any video manually?
- Will I be streaming from multiple sources?
- What kind of design do I want?

- Will I include any other types of content on my site?

- How will I record and upload my videos?

- Who is my target audience and how will I reach them?

- Do I want to make money from my videos?

- How often will I create videos and what will my recording and editing process be?

- What software and hardware will I need for recording and editing videos?

It's beyond the scope of this chapter to answer all of these questions, but it's worth taking some time before you start to consider how you're going to be using your video site, what you'll be adding to it, and what your objectives are.

Streaming from YouTube or uploading videos directly?

WordPress lets you upload your videos directly to your site using the **Add Media** button, the same button you use to insert images. This can seem like the simplest way of doing things as you only need to work in one place.

However, I would strongly recommend using a third-party video service instead, for the following reasons:

- It saves on storage space in your site.

- It ensures that your videos will play on any device people choose to view your site from.

- It keeps the formats your video is played in up to date so that you don't have to re-upload them when things change.

- It can have massive SEO benefits socially if you use YouTube. YouTube is owned by Google and has excellent search engine rankings. You'll find that videos streamed via YouTube get better Google rankings than any videos you upload directly to your site.

In this chapter, the focus will be on creating a YouTube channel and streaming video from it to your website. We'll set things up so that when you add new videos to your channel, they'll be automatically streamed to your site. To do that, we'll use a plugin.

Understanding copyright considerations

Before you start uploading video to YouTube, you need to understand what you're allowed to add, and how copyright affects your videos.

You can find plenty of information on YouTube's copyright rules and processes at `https://www.youtube.com/yt/copyright/`, but it can quite easily be summarized as this: if you created the video, or it was created by someone who has given you explicit permission to use it and publish it online, then you can upload it. If you've recorded a video from the TV or the Web that you didn't make and don't have permission to reproduce (or if you've added copyrighted music to your own videos without permission), then you can't upload it.

It may seem tempting to ignore copyright and upload anything you're able to find and record (and you'll find plenty of examples of people who've done just that), but you are running a risk of being prosecuted for copyright infringement and being forced to pay a huge fine.

I'd also suggest that if you can create and publish original video content rather than copying someone else's, you'll find an audience of fans for that content, and it will be a much more enjoyable process.

If your videos involve screen capture of you using software or playing games, you'll need to check the license for that software or game to be sure that you're entitled to publish video of you interacting with it. Most software and games developers have no problem with this as it provides free advertising for them, but you should check with the software provider and the YouTube copyright advice. Movies and music have stricter rules than games generally do, however. If you upload videos containing someone else's video or music content that's copyrighted and you haven't got permission to reproduce it, you will find yourself in violation of YouTube's rules and possibly in legal trouble too.

Creating a YouTube channel and uploading videos

So, you've planned your channel and you have some videos you want to share with the world. You'll need a YouTube channel so you can upload your videos.

Creating your YouTube channel

Let's create a YouTube channel by following these steps:

1. If you don't already have one, create a Google account for yourself at `https://accounts.google.com/SignUp`.

2. Head over to YouTube at `https://www.youtube.com` and sign in. You'll have an account with YouTube because it's part of Google, but you won't have a channel yet.

3. Go to `https://www.youtube.com/channel_switcher`. Click on the **Create a new channel** button.

4. Follow the instructions on screen to create your channel.

5. Customize your channel by uploading images to your profile photo or channel art and adding a description using the **About** tab.

Here's my channel:

Fig 5.1: The new channel with artwork

 It can take a while for artwork from Google+ to show up on your channel, so don't worry if you don't see it straight away.

Uploading videos

The next step is to upload some videos. YouTube accepts videos in the following formats:

- .MOV
- .MPEG4
- .AVI
- .WMV
- .MPEGPS
- .FLV
- 3GPP
- WebM

Depending on the video software you've used to record, your video may already be in one of these formats, or you may need to export it to one of these and save it before you can upload it.

If you're not sure how to convert your file to one of the supported formats, you'll find advice at `https://support.google.com/youtube/troubleshooter/2888402` to help you do it.

 You can also upload videos to YouTube directly from your phone or tablet. On an Android device, you'll need to use the YouTube app, while on an iOS device you can log in to YouTube on the device and upload from the camera app. For detailed instructions and advice for other devices, refer to `https://support.google.com/youtube/answer/57407`.

If you're uploading directly to the YouTube website, simply click on the **Upload** button when viewing your channel and follow the onscreen instructions. Make sure you add your video to a playlist by clicking on the **+Add to playlist** button on the right-hand side while you're setting up the video as this will help you categorize the videos in your site later.

Now when you open your channel page and click on the **Videos** tab, you'll see all the videos you uploaded:

Fig 5.2: Uploaded videos on YouTube

When you click on the **Playlists** tab, you'll see your new playlist:

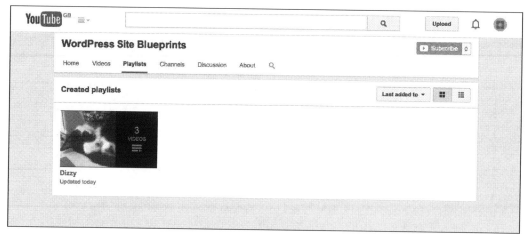

Fig 5.3: The playlist on YouTube

So you now have some videos and a playlist set up in YouTube. It's time to set up your WordPress site for streaming those videos.

Installing and configuring the YouTube plugin

Now that you have your videos and playlists set up, it's time to add a plugin to your site that will automatically add new videos to your site when you upload them to YouTube.

Because I've created a playlist, I'm going to use a category in my site for the playlist and automatically add new videos to that category as posts. If you prefer, you can use different channels for each category or you can just use one video category and link your channel to that. The latter is useful if your site will contain other content as well, such as photos or blog posts.

Note that you don't need a plugin to stream YouTube videos to your site. You can simply paste the URL for a video into the editing pane when you're creating a post or page in your site, and WordPress will automatically stream the video. You don't even need to add an embed code, just add the URL. If you don't want to automate the process of streaming all of the videos in your channel to your site, this plugin will make that process easy.

Installing the Automatic YouTube Video Posts plugin

The **Automatic YouTube Video Posts** plugin lets you link your site to any YouTube channel or playlist and automatically adds each new video to your site as a post. Let's start by installing it.

I'm working with a fresh WordPress installation, but you can also do this on your existing site if that's what you're working with. Follow these steps:

1. In the WordPress admin, go to **Plugins | Add New**.
2. In the **Search Plugin** box, type `Automatic Youtube`.
3. The plugins that meet the search criteria will be displayed. Select the **Automatic YouTube Video Posts Plugin** and then install and activate it.

For the plugin to work, you'll need to configure its settings and add one or more channels or playlists.

Configuring the plugin settings

Let's start with the plugin's settings screen. You do this via the **Youtube Posts** menu, which the plugin has added to your admin menu:

1. Go to **Youtube Posts | Settings**.

2. Edit the settings as follows:

   ° **Automatically publish posts**: Set this to **yes**

   ° **Display YouTube video meta**: Set this to **yes**

   ° **Number of words before WordPress' "More" tag** and **Video dimensions**: Leave these at the default values

   ° **Display related videos**: Set this to **no**

   ° **Display videos in post lists**: Set this to **yes**

   ° **Import the latest videos every**: Set this to **1 hours** (note that the updates will happen every hour if someone visits the site, but not if the site isn't visited)

3. Click on the **Save Changes** button.

The settings screen will look similar to the following screenshot:

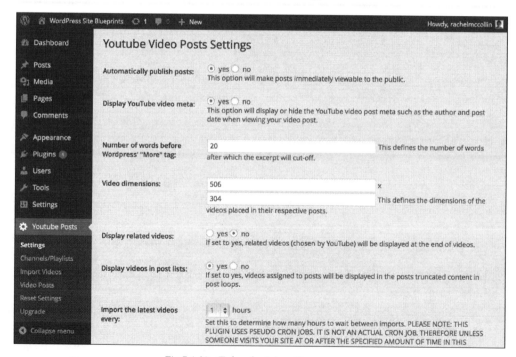

Fig 5.4: YouTube plugin's settings screen

Adding a YouTube channel or playlist

The next step is to add a YouTube channel and/or playlist so that the plugin will create posts from your videos. I'm going to add the "Dizzy" playlist that I created earlier on, but first, I'll create a category for all my videos from that playlist.

Creating a category for a playlist

Create a category for your playlist in the normal way:

1. In the WordPress admin, go to **Posts | Categories**.
2. Add the category name and slug or description if you want to (if you don't, WordPress will automatically create a slug).
3. Click on the **Add New Category** button.

Adding your channel or playlist to the plugin

Now you need to configure the plugin so that it creates posts in the category you've just created.

1. In the WordPress admin, go to **Youtube Posts | Channels/Playlists**.
2. Click on the **Add New** button.
3. Add the details of your channel or playlist, as shown in the next screenshot. In my case, the details are as follows:
   - **Name**: Dizzy
   - **Channel/playlist**: This is the ID of my playlist. To find this, open the playlist in YouTube and then copy the last part of its URL from your browser. The URL for my playlist is `https://www.youtube.com/watch?v=vd128vVQc6Y&list=PLG9W2ELAaa-Wh6sVbQAIB9RtN_1UV49Uv` and the playlist ID is after the `&list=` text, so it's `PLG9W2ELAaa-Wh6sVbQAIB9RtN_1UV49Uv`. If you want to add a channel, add its unique name.
   - **Type**: Select **Channel** or **Playlist**; I'm selecting **Playlist**.
   - **Add videos from this channel/playlist to the following categories**: Select the category you just created.
   - **Attribute videos from this channel to what author**: Select the author whom you want to attribute videos to, if your site has more than one author.

4. Finally, click on the **Add Channel** button.

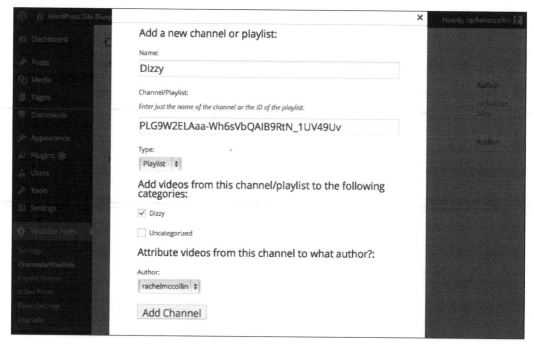

Fig 5.5: Adding a YouTube playlist

Once you click on the **Add Channel** button, you'll be taken back to the **Channels/Playlists** screen, where you'll see your playlist or channel added:

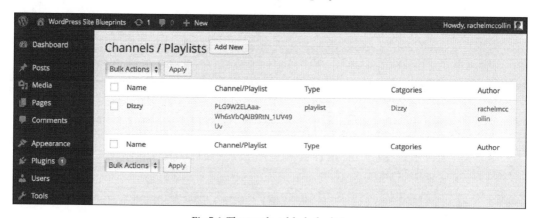

Fig 5.6: The newly added playlist

If you like, you can add more channels or playlists and more categories.

Now go to the **Posts** listing screen in your WordPress admin, and you'll see that the plugin has created posts for each of the videos in your playlist:

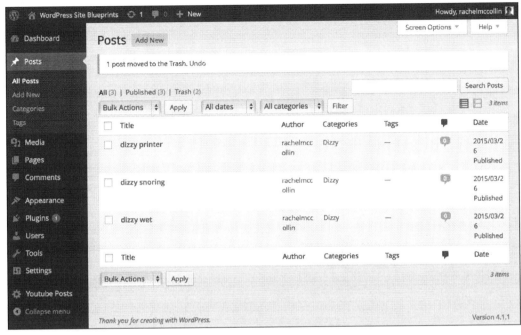

Fig 5.7: Automatically added posts

Installing and configuring a suitable theme

You'll need a suitable theme in your site to make your videos stand out. I'm going to use the Keratin theme which is grid-based with a right-hand sidebar. A grid-based theme works well as people can see your videos on your home page and category pages.

Installing the theme

Let's install the theme:

1. Go to **Appearance | Themes**.
2. Click on the **Add New** button.
3. In the search box, type Keratin.
4. The theme will be listed. Click on the **Install** button.
5. When prompted, click on the **Activate** button.

The theme will now be displayed in your admin screen as active:

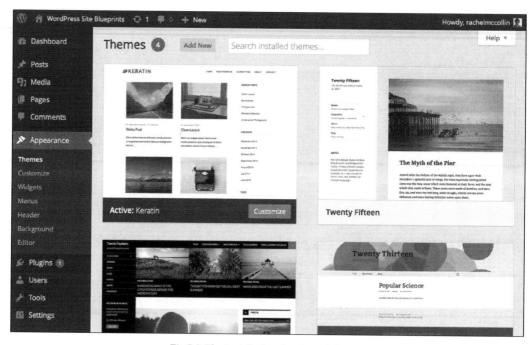

Fig 5.8: The installed and activated theme

Creating a navigation menu

Now that you've activated a new theme, you'll need to make sure your navigation menu is configured so that it's in the theme's primary menu slot, or if you haven't created a menu yet, you'll need to create one. Follow these steps:

1. Go to **Appearance | Menus**.

2. If you don't already have a menu, click on the **create a new menu** link, name your new menu, and click on the **Create Menu** button.

3. Add your home page to the menu along with any category pages you've created by clicking on the **Categories** metabox on the left-hand side.

4. Once everything is in the right place in your menu, click on the **Save Menu** button.

Your **Menus** screen will look something similar to this:

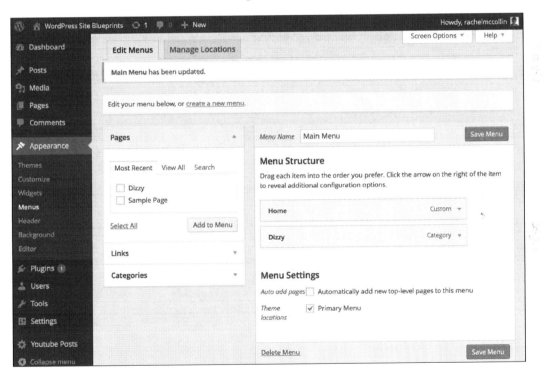

Fig 5.9: The Menus screen

Now that you have a menu, let's take a look at the site:

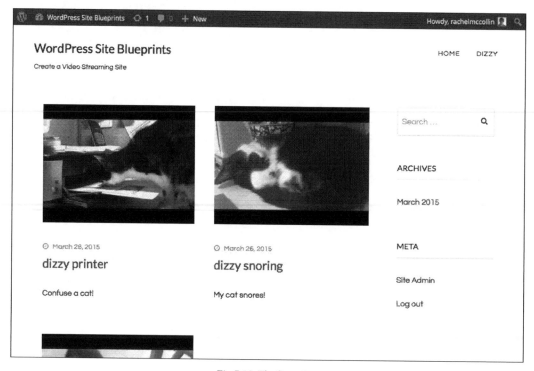

Fig 5.10: The live site

That's looking good, but I'd like to add some text in the sidebar instead of the default content.

Adding a text widget to the sidebar

Let's add a text widget with some information about the site:

1. In the WordPress admin, go to **Appearance | Widgets**.
2. Find the text widget on the left-hand side and drag it into the widget area for the main sidebar.
3. Give the widget a title.

4. Type the following text into the widget's contents: Welcome to this video site. To see my videos on YouTube, visit https://www.youtube.com/ channel/UC5NPnKZOjCxhPBLZn_DHOMw. Replace the link I've added here with a link to your own channel:

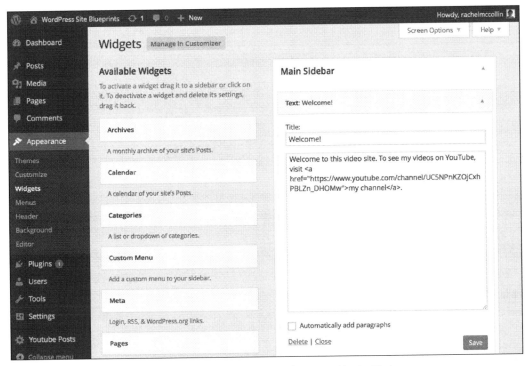

Fig 5.11: The Widgets screen with a text widget added

Text widgets accept text and HTML. Here we've used HTML to create a link. For more on HTML links, visit http://www.w3schools.com/ html/html_links.asp. Alternatively, if you'd rather create a widget that gives you an editing pane like the one you use for creating posts, you can install the TinyMCE Widget plugin from https://wordpress. org/plugins/black-studio-tinymce-widget/screenshots/. This gives you a widget that lets you create links and format your text just as you would when creating a post.

5. Now go back to your live site to see how things are looking:

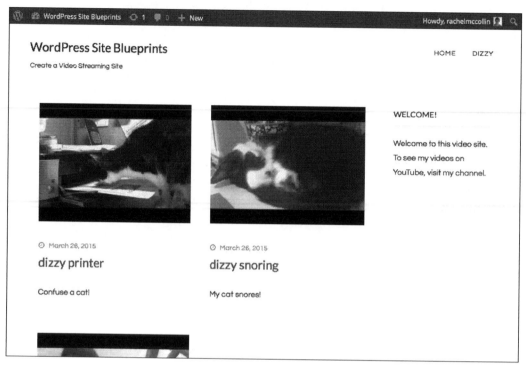

Fig 5.12: The live site with a text widget added

It's looking much better!

If you click on one of these videos, you're taken to the post for that video:

Fig 5.13: A single post with a video automatically added

Your site is now ready.

Managing and updating your videos

The great thing about using this plugin is that once you've set it up, you'll never have to do anything in your website to add new videos. All you need to do is upload them to YouTube and add them to the playlist you've linked to, and they'll automatically be added to your site.

If you want to add extra content to the posts holding your videos, you can do so. Just edit the posts in the normal way, adding text, images, and anything you want. These will be displayed as well as the videos.

If you want to create new playlists in future, you just do this in YouTube and then create a new category on your site and add the playlist in the settings for the plugin, assigning the new channel to the relevant category.

You can upload your videos to YouTube in a variety of ways—via the YouTube website or directly from the device or software that you used to record and/or edit them. Most phones allow you to sign in to your YouTube account via the video or YouTube app and directly upload videos, and video editing software will often let you do the same.

Good luck with your video site, I hope it gets you lots of views!

Summary

In this chapter, you learned how to create a WordPress site for streaming video from YouTube. You created a YouTube channel and added videos and playlists to it and then you set up your site to automatically create a new post each time you add a new video, using a plugin. Finally, you installed a suitable theme and configured it, creating categories for your channels and adding these to your navigation menu.

6
Creating a Review Site

More and more of us are turning to the Internet before making purchasing decisions. We seek out reviews of products and services before buying and are reliant not only on the opinions of expert reviewers, but also of other members of the public who've bought the product or used the service we're interested in.

If you want to create a community site or any kind of listings site, or even a store, it will provide another level of interaction for your users if you let them leave reviews. These reviews could be of the products you're selling or reviewing yourself, or of local businesses and services.

In this chapter, I'll show you how to create a site designed to let users review local restaurants. We'll set up the site with a suitable theme and some posts for the restaurants and then use a plugin to let users leave reviews on the site. You'll learn how to administer reviews and publish them on the site so that future visitors can see them. Finally, we'll add maps to the site so that users can find the restaurants they're reading about.

So let's get started!

Planning your review site

Before you set up your review site, I'd advise you to take some time to plan how it will work and what you want people to be able to review.

Here are some questions you might ask yourself:

- Will people be allowed to post reviews or just give ratings?
- Do users have to subscribe to the site and log in to leave reviews?
- Do you want to create your own in-depth reviews and maybe let users add their own too?

- What kind of product or service will people be reviewing?
- If you're including multiple types of products or services, how do you need to structure your site to accommodate these? Think about whether you need custom post types or taxonomies (for more on custom post types and taxonomies, see later in this chapter).

These are just a few questions that will help you plan your site. The main thing you need to consider is whether your site is for reviews or just ratings. Let me explain the difference:

- A reviews site lets people post text-based reviews, as well as (optionally) gives a rating. This has the advantage of providing readers with more in-depth information.
- A ratings site just lets people give a star rating and doesn't let them add any text. This has the advantage of letting users see aggregated scores for items, but doesn't give more useful information to back up those scores.

In this chapter, we'll create a reviews site. This site will let users add a star rating to each post on the site and add a text-based review too. It will let anyone post a review, but we'll manage reviews and approve them before publishing them. It will be a review site for local restaurants, letting people find restaurants by category and leave reviews of them.

The first step in doing all this is to create the site and install a suitable theme.

Creating the site and installing a theme

You might be working on a site you've already created, but I'm working on a brand new WordPress installation so I need to install a theme before I get started. If you're doing the same, follow these steps:

1. Create your site and install WordPress in the usual way. If you're unsure about this, take a look at *Chapter 1, Migrating a Static Site to WordPress*.
2. Go to **Appearance | Themes**.
3. Click on the **Add New** button.

4. Find a suitable theme by typing one or more search terms in the search box. We're going to use the Baskerville theme, which you can find at `https://wordpress.org/themes/baskerville/` or by typing `Baskerville` into the search box.

5. After you've searched for the theme, it will be displayed on your screen. Click on the **Install** button to install it on your site.

6. On the **Installing Theme** page, click on the **Activate** button to activate the new theme.

7. The theme will now be active on your site:

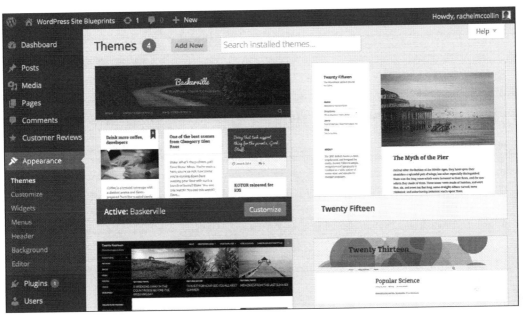

Fig 6.1: The theme installed on your site

Now that you have the theme installed, you can use the theme customizer to make some customizations to the colors and fonts if you like. Go to **Appearance** | **Customize** and tweak the settings however you'd like. I'm just going to change some of the colors.

Installing the WP Customer Reviews plugin

The next step is to install the plugin that will enable reviews. The plugin we're using here is the **WP Customer Reviews** plugin. This lets your site visitors rate individual posts and leave reviews. It automatically holds new reviews as pending until you've approved them and then it publishes them in the post where they were added. Follow these steps:

1. Go to **Plugins | Add New**.

2. In the search box, type WP Customer Reviews.

3. The plugin will be displayed. Click on the **Install Now** button to install it in your site.

4. When prompted, click on the **Activate** link to activate it.

Configuring the plugin's settings

The plugin only has one settings screen as most of the work is done in the editing screen for individual posts.

Go to **Settings | Customer Reviews** to view the **Options** screen:

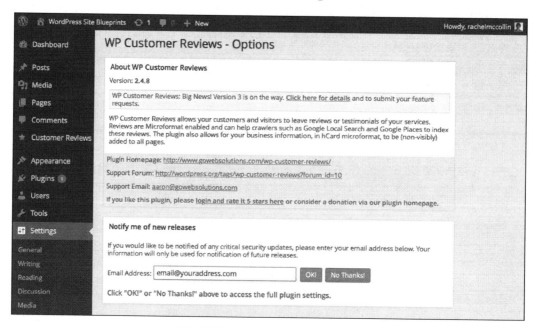

Fig 6.2: The WP Customer Reviews - Options screen

If you want to receive notifications of updates to the plugin, insert your e-mail address in the field as I've done in the preceding screenshot and click on the **OK!** button.

That's it! You don't need to do anything else to configure the plugin. But, before we start adding posts for people to review, let's configure the site's discussion settings.

Configuring the discussion settings

Before adding any posts and setting up reviews, it's a good idea to edit the discussion settings for the site. As we'll be allowing people to post reviews on our posts, we don't want to allow comments as well as that would create confusion. If we switch this off now, the change will apply to all posts we create from now on. Follow these steps:

1. Go to **Settings | Discussion**.
2. In the **Default article settings** section, uncheck the **Allow people to post comments on new articles** button.
3. Scroll down the screen and click on the **Save Changes** button.

You can see this in the following screenshot:

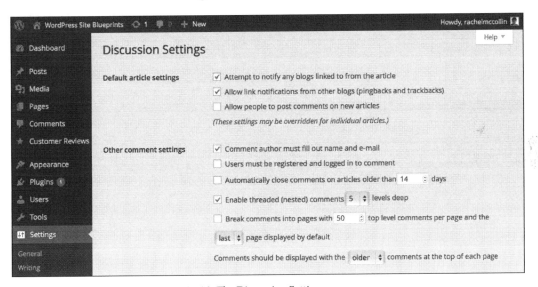

Fig 6.3: The Discussion Settings screen

If you've already created some posts in your review site, you'll have to go into each post and turn off comments. Scroll down to the **Discussion** metabox and uncheck the **Allow comments** checkbox. If you can't see the **Discussion** metabox, click on the **Screen Options** tab at the top of the screen and check the box for that metabox. If you've added a lot of posts and want to quickly turn off comments for all of them, you can use the **Disable Comments** plugin to disable comments for all the existing posts. You can download it from `https://wordpress.org/plugins/disable-comments/` or install it as you would install any plugin. If you're allowing comments, make sure you've got the Akismet plugin enabled, which come preinstalled with WordPress.

Viewing reviews

Once you've installed the plugin, you can view all the reviews that have been posted at any time. Do this by clicking on **Customer Reviews** in the admin menu, to see the **Pending Reviews** screen:

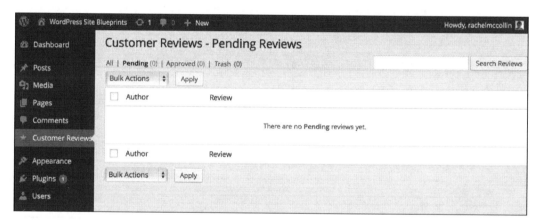

Fig 6.4: The Pending Reviews screen

From here, you can manage all of the reviews that have been posted, including approving them, trashing them, and even deleting them.

We'll return to this screen later on after the first review has been posted.

Creating posts for our review site

Before anyone can post a review, we need something for them to review!

In this site, I'm going to use a post for each restaurant that people will be able to review. If you're already using posts for your blog, you might want to create a separate post type for the products or services you want people to review.

> If you want to create custom post types, you can do so using a plugin or by writing code in your theme. A plugin that will help you do this is the Custom Post Type UI plugin, available at `https://wordpress.org/plugins/custom-post-type-ui/`. For a guide to coding the post types yourself, visit `http://premium.wpmudev.org/blog/creating-content-custom-post-types/`.

Creating the posts

I'm going to create a post for each restaurant in my site. Go ahead and create a number of posts for your review site in the same way.

The following screenshot shows all my posts. As you can see, I've added them to categories relating to the type of cuisine offered by each restaurant:

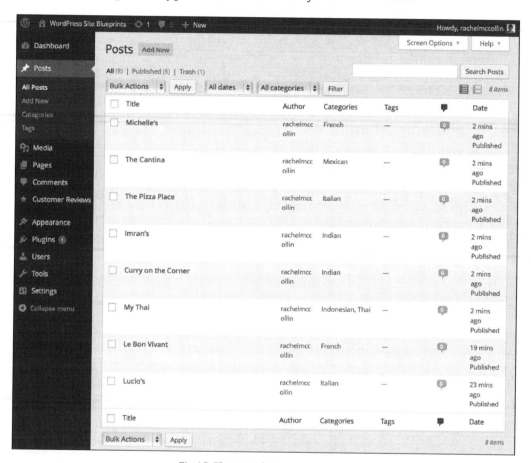

Fig 6.5: The posts for our review site

Now we need to enable reviews of those posts.

Enabling reviews for posts

At the moment, people won't be able to add any reviews to the posts in the site. With the **Customer Reviews** plugin, we need to enable them for each post that we want reviews to be added to. This gives us a lot of flexibility as it means that if you don't want to add reviews to all of your posts or post types, you just don't enable them for those posts. However, it does mean that you have to remember to enable reviews for each new review post that you create. Follow these steps:

1. Open one of your posts.

2. Scroll down the screen to the **WP Customer Reviews** metabox, as shown in the following screenshot. If you can't see this metabox, open the **Screen Options** tab at the top of the screen to enable it.

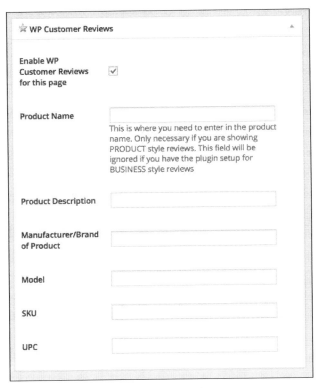

Fig 6.6: Enabling reviews for a post

3. Check the **Enable WP Customer Reviews for this page** checkbox.

4. Update your changes by clicking on the **Update** button for the post.

Note that we left all of the other fields in the **WP Customer Reviews** metabox empty. This is because people will be leaving reviews on the post itself, and not on a product.

Now let's take a look at the post with reviews enabled:

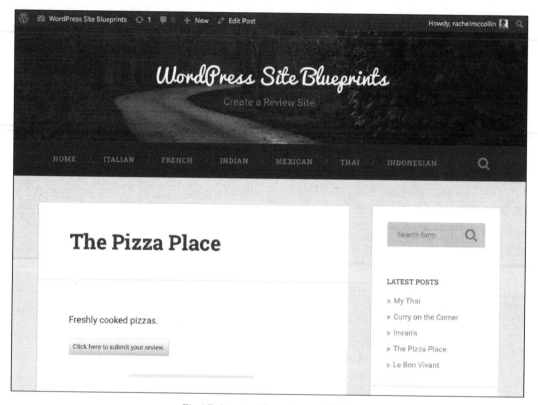

Fig 6.7: A post with reviews enabled

The plugin adds a button to the page so that people can submit reviews.

Submitting reviews

When a user clicks on the button for submitting reviews, they'll be shown an interface that they can use for leaving their review, as shown in the following screenshot:

Fig 6.8: The review interface for users

In the preceding screenshot, you can see that I've created a review in just the same way your users would do.

Try creating a few reviews now, on different pages in your site, and submitting them.

When you submit your review, it won't automatically be published. This is because you need to moderate each review that's left before publishing it to your site.

Instead, users will see a message telling them what will happen:

Fig 6.9: A message tells people submitting reviews that their review will be moderated

So, the next step is for you to moderate those reviews.

Moderating and publishing reviews

When a user leaves a review, the site admin (that's you) will automatically receive an e-mail, notifying them of the new review.

You need to log in to your site and view new reviews in order to approve them and publish them to the site. This prevents people from posting spammy or inappropriate reviews.

Do you remember the empty **Pending Reviews** screen that we looked at earlier? That's the screen we'll be using again now. Follow these steps:

In the WordPress admin menu, click on **Customer Reviews**. You'll see the new review that's been posted, as shown in the following screenshot:

Fig 6.10: The Pending Reviews screen with new reviews displayed

Take action on the review in one of the following ways:

- To approve a review, simply hover over it and click on the **Mark as Approved** link
- If you get a review that you don't want to publish, click on the **Move to Trash** or **Delete Forever** links.
- If you want to reply to the review, type your response in the **Official Response** field

WordPress will automatically publish, trash, or delete the review, and add your response if you left one.

The following screenshot shows how my review looks once it's been approved and published:

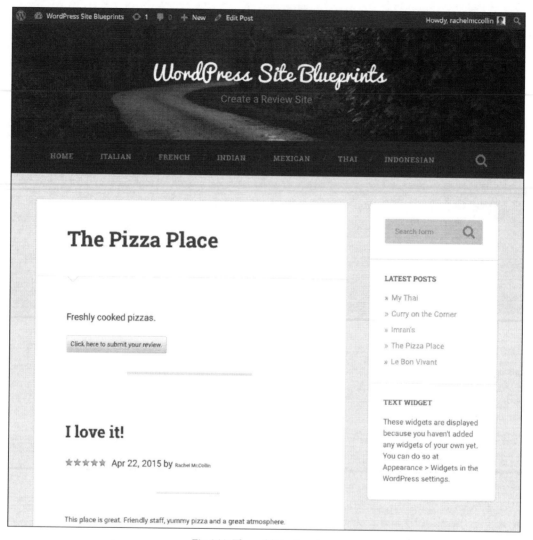

Fig 6.11: The published review

Now all of your users can see the reviews that other users have left and you've approved. So, you now have reviews set up on your site and you know how to administer them. As this is a restaurant site, let's add an extra layer of helpfulness for our users by incorporating maps.

Adding maps to our review site

If you're creating a review site for local businesses (such as restaurants), including maps will make your site more helpful for users and encourage them to come back regularly.

You could do this by going to Google maps and copying the embedded code for a location's map into your post, but the good news is that you can make this easier with a WordPress plugin called **CP Google Maps**.

This plugin lets you create a map on each post or page in your site. There are lots of Google maps plugins out there, but you'll find that a lot of them require you to create the maps separately and then add them to your posts using a short code. This plugin makes things easier by letting you do everything in one place when you're creating your posts.

Installing the CP Google Maps plugin

First, let's install the plugin:

1. Go to **Plugins | Add New**.
2. In the search box, type CP Google Maps.
3. When the plugin appears, click on the **Install Now** button.
4. When prompted, click on the **Activate** link.

Now that the plugin's installed, it's time to configure it.

Configuring the CP Google Maps plugin

Before adding any maps, you'll need to configure the plugin's settings:

1. Go to **Settings | CodePeople Post Map**.
2. Make any changes to the settings you need for your site. I'm going to change two settings:
    ◦ **Map zoom**: Set at 15 to have the maps zoomed in a bit more than the default
    ◦ **Map width**: Change this to 100% to make the maps responsive for smaller screens
3. Scroll down and click on the **Update Settings** button to save your changes.

You can see the settings in the following screenshot:

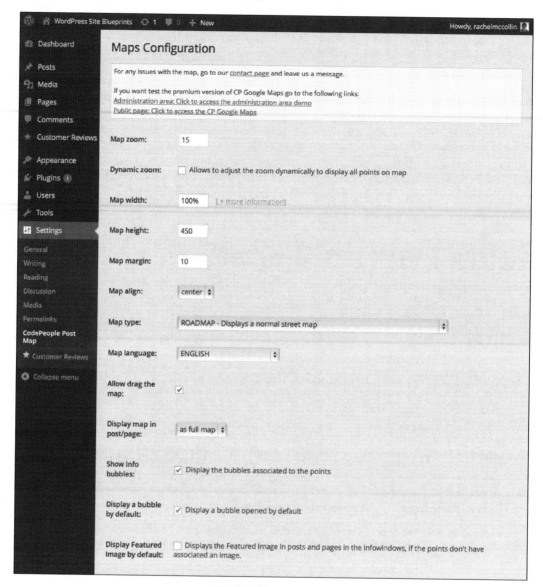

Fig 6.12: Maps settings

Now that you have the plugin configured, it's time to add a map.

Adding maps to posts

You can add a map to each of your posts with this plugin. Follow these steps:

1. Open one of your posts.
2. Scroll down to the **Maps** metabox, as shown in the following screenshot. Again, if you can't see the metabox, enable it using the **Screen Options** tab.

Fig 6.13: The Maps metabox

3. Complete the fields as follows:

   ○ **Location name and Location description**: These are optional and will take up space on the map. I've left them blank as it's pretty obvious that this is a map of the restaurant that the post relates to.

   ○ **Select an image**: Leave this blank as we'll use one of the markers provided by Google maps.

   ○ **Address**: Type in the address of the location here. The **Latitude** and **Longitude** fields will automatically be filled when Google maps identifies your address. If it can't find your address, you'll have to enter the latitude and longitude manually.

4. Click on the **Verify** button to verify your address.

5. Select a marker from the ones provided. I've chosen the familiar balloon marker.

6. Save the changes to your post by clicking on the **Update** button.

After saving your post, let's see how it looks on the site:

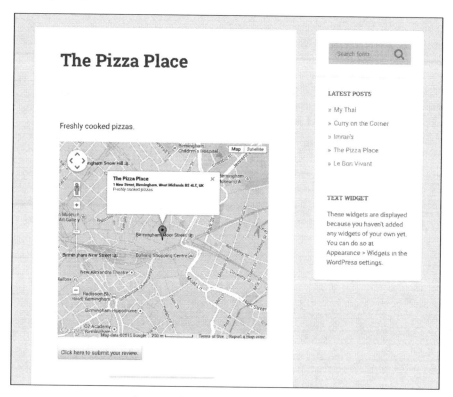

Fig 6.14: The map on the site's frontend

That looks good! Hopefully, it will help your site's visitors to find the restaurants that they've read reviews of and make the site even more useful.

Tidying up the site – adding widgets

All of the content and settings for our review site are now in place. Each post has reviews enabled and a map of the location it relates to.

Let's just finish things up by adding some widgets to the footer of our site:

1. In the WordPress admin, go to **Appearance | Widgets**.

2. Delete any widgets that WordPress has added by default.

3. Add the following widgets to the footer widget areas, as shown in the following screenshot:

    ○ **Recent posts**

    ○ **Categories**

    ○ **Search**

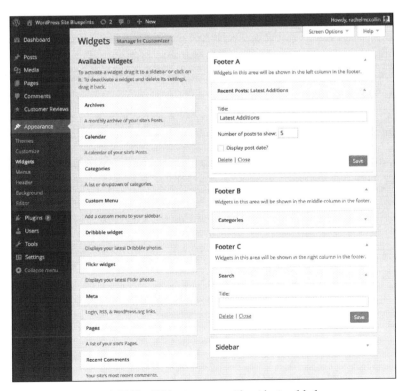

Fig 6.15: The Widgets screen with widgets added

These widgets will help people navigate around your site and view the most recently added posts. Here's how they look on the site.

Fig 6.16: The widgets in the footer

Summary

A review site will provide a useful resource for visitors. The site you've created in this chapter allows people to post restaurant reviews and also provides maps to help them find those restaurants.

In this chapter, you learned how to install and configure a plugin to enable reviews, create posts for reviews, add some reviews and administer them, and add a plugin to insert a map in each post and add maps to each post.

Well done! Don't forget to keep your review site updated and add new restaurants when they open. Good luck!

In the next chapter, you'll learn how to create something more serious—a jobs board. You'll install a plugin and create a site to list jobs that people can apply for online.

7
Creating a Jobs Board

These days, very few people apply for a job by posting their CV off to a company; instead, they search and apply for jobs online. Jobs board sites have become huge, with thousands, if not millions, of people using them to get work and thousands of employers using them to find talent.

This doesn't just apply to full time jobs; freelancers and people looking for short term work also use jobs boards to find work.

The great news is that WordPress makes it easy for you to create your own jobs board. If you're running a blog or site aimed at a specific industry or sector, you can add a jobs board to it as an extra resource for your readers. Alternatively, you can create a site comprised of just a jobs board, maybe to serve a local community or a specific sector.

In this chapter, I'll show you how to do this. We'll install and configure the WP Job Manager plugin and set up a suitable theme. Next, we'll add some jobs both via the admin screens and frontend of the site and see how to search for jobs and apply for them.

Planning your jobs board

If you're going to create a jobs board site, you need to put some thought into how it will work, what its target audience will be, and what they'll be able to get from it.

Here are some questions you might ask yourself:

- Is the jobs board the sole purpose of the site or is it part of a blog or other kind of site?
- What is the audience for the jobs board? Consider employers and applicants too.

- How will you advertise your jobs board and encourage employers to post jobs on it?

- Do you intend to make money from your jobs board? If so, will this be via advertising or by charging employers for posting jobs?

- Will people apply for jobs on your site or on the employers' sites?

In this chapter, we're going to build a standalone jobs board that doesn't include application forms; applicants will click a link to go to the employer's site or e-mail a CV to them.

I'm going to populate my jobs board with some dummy jobs in web design and content creation, but your jobs could be anything you want.

Installing and configuring the WP Job Manager plugin

The first step is to install and configure the plugin that we'll be using to manage jobs. This is the free WP Job Manager plugin, which you can find in the official WordPress plugin repository at https://wordpress.org/plugins/wp-job-manager/.

I'm assuming that you've already set up WordPress; if you need to do this first and you're not sure where to start from, refer to *Chapter 1, Migrating a Static Site to WordPress.*

Installing the WP Job Manager plugin

First things first, let's install the plugin:

1. In your WordPress admin, go to **Plugins | Add New**.
2. In the search box, type WP Job Manager.
3. From the plugins that WordPress selected for you, select the **WP Job Manager** plugin and click on the **Install Now** button.
4. When the plugin is installed, click on the **Activate** link.

The plugin is now active on your site. Before adding any jobs, however, you need to configure it.

Configuring the WP Job Manager plugin

Having installed the plugin, it's time to set it up.

Adding pages

The first step is to add pages to hold job details by following these steps:

1. When you activate the plugin, you'll be taken to the setup screen (if you're not, go to **Job Listings | Settings** to access it):

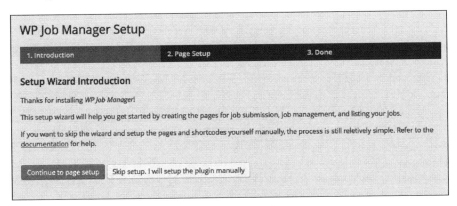

Fig 7.1: The WP Job Manager Setup screen

2. Click on the **Continue to page setup** button.

   Now you'll see the **Page Setup** screen, as shown in the following screenshot:

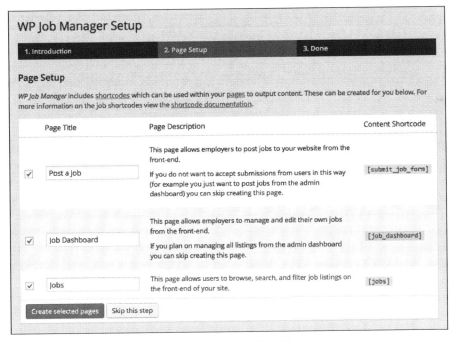

Fig 7.2: The WP Job Manager's Page Setup screen

3. Make sure each of the checkboxes is ticked, and click the **Create selected pages** button.

The plugin will create the pages for your job listings, tell you that everything's done, and provide you with some useful links:

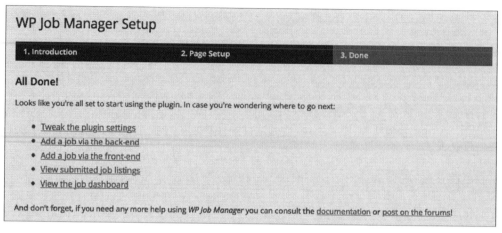

Fig 7.3: The Page Setup process is complete

The plugin has created four new pages for you, each of which will be used to display jobs. Take a look at your pages in the admin if you want to check them out.

 If you want to add job listings to pages you've already created on your site, you can do this by adding the short codes provided by the plugin to those pages. They're shown in Fig 7.2.

Configuring Job Listings

Now let's configure the rest of the plugin settings. First up is **Job Listings**:

1. Go to **Job Listings | Settings** to view the **Job Listings** setup screen:
2. Configure the settings as follows:
    ° **Listings Per Page**: Choose what works for you. I'm typing 10.
    ° **Filled Positions**: Check the box to hide positions that have been filled.
    ° **Expired Listings**: Check the box to hide listings whose deadline for applications has passed.
    ° **Categories**: Check the box to enable job categories. We'll add some of these shortly.

○ **Multi-select Categories**: Check the box to enable this so that people looking for jobs aren't limited to searching for just one category.

○ **Category Filter Type**: Select **Jobs will be shown if within ANY selected category**.

The screen will look something similar to this:

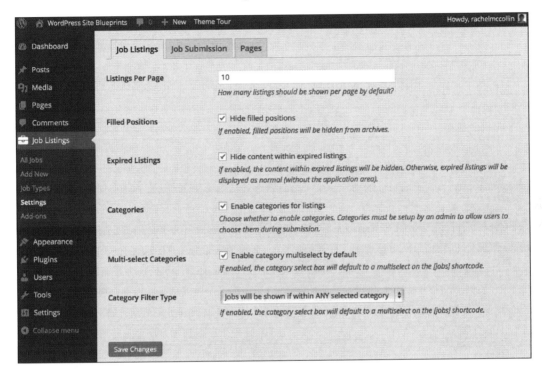

Fig 7.4: The Job Listings configuration screen

3. Click on the **Save Changes** button.

Configuring Job Submission

Now let's configure the way jobs are submitted:

1. Still in the WP Job Manager settings screens, click on the **Job Submission** tab.

2. Configure the settings as follows:

○ **Account Required**: Check the box to force users to create an account in order to post a job listing. This will help you with communications and marketing, and will reduce spam.

○ **Account Creation**: Check the box to let job posters create an account.

- ○ **Account Username**: Check the box to automatically generate a username for new accounts.

- ○ **Account Role**: Select **Employer**. This is an additional WordPress user role created by the plugin.

- ○ **Moderate New Listings**: Check the box to stop new listings being posted until you've moderated them.

- ○ **Allow Pending Edits**: Uncheck this box.

- ○ **Listing Duration**: Type 30 to have jobs expire automatically after 30 days.

- ○ **Application Method**: Select **Email address or website URL**.

The screen will look similar to this:

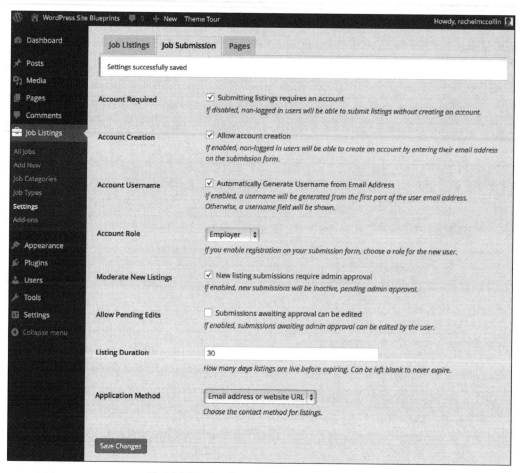

Fig 7.5: The Job Submission configuration screen

3. Click on the **Save Changes** button to save what you've done.

Configuring pages

Finally, we need to configure the pages by following these steps:

1. Still in the WP Job Manager settings screens, click on the **Pages** tab.

2. Configure the settings like this:

   ◦ **Submit Job Form Page**: Select **Post a Job**

   ◦ **Job Dashboard Page**: Select **Job Dashboard**

   ◦ **Job Listings Page**: Select **Jobs**

   The settings will look similar to the following screenshot:

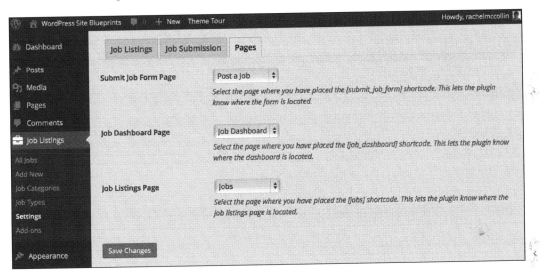

Fig 7.6: The Pages configuration screen

3. Click on the **Save Changes** button.

Creating Job Categories

Now that the settings are in place for the plugin, let's create some job categories:

1. Go to **Job Listings | Job Categories**.

2. Add the categories you're going to use for your jobs. You can see mine in the following screenshot:

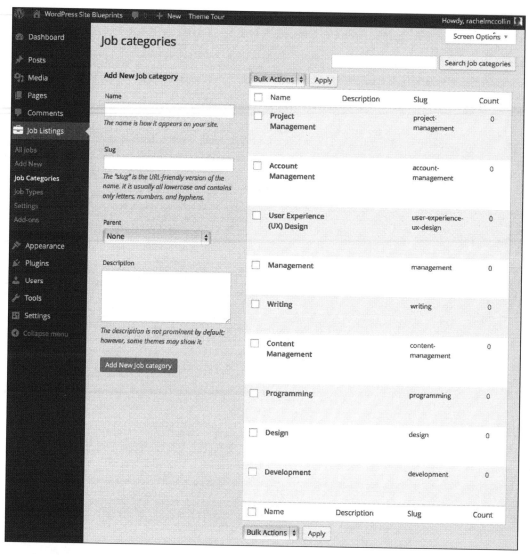

Fig 7.7: The Job categories screen

Defining the front page

As this site is just for job listings, we want the **Jobs** page to be the front page. Let's set that up:

1. Go to **Settings | Reading**.

2. In the **Front page displays** section, select **A static page**. In the **Front page** drop-down list, select **Jobs**. Don't select anything for the **Posts page** (unless you're already running a blog on this site):

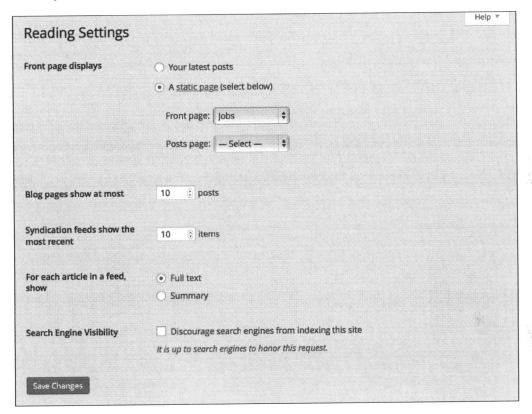

Fig 7.8: Front page settings

3. Click on the **Save Changes** button.

That's all! The plugin configuration is complete. Let's move on to the next step.

Installing and configuring a theme

To make your jobs site look as good as possible and easy to find, and navigate around job listings, we need a suitable theme. If you've already got a theme you're using, you don't need to worry about this, but if you're working with a clean WordPress installation, read on!

Installing the Vantage theme

Let's install the Vantage theme. It's a clean, modern theme with some nice configuration options. You could use any theme you like; this one isn't designed for jobs boards, but I think its design works well with the jobs board layout. Follow these steps:

1. In the WordPress admin, go to **Appearance | Themes**.

2. Click on the **Add New** button.

3. In the search box, type Vantage.

4. WordPress will display all the themes matching your search terms. Select **Vantage** and click on the **Install** button.

5. Once the theme has been installed, click on the **Activate** button.

The theme will now be active:

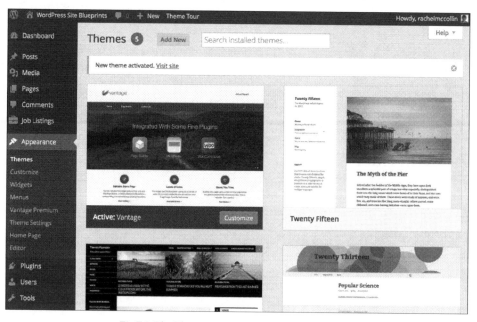

Fig 7.9: The Themes screen with Vantage activated

Configuring Theme Settings

The Vantage theme comes with a few settings, which you can experiment with until the site looks as you want it to. However, I'm only going to change one setting and that relates to the front page slider, which I don't want on my site:

1. Go to **Appearance | Theme Settings**.

2. Click on the **Home** tab.

3. In the **Home Page Slider** drop-down box, select **None**, as shown in the following screenshot:

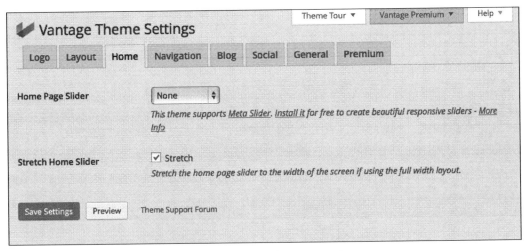

Fig 7.10: The theme's front page settings

4. Click on the **Save Settings** button.

Creating a menu

Next, we need to create a navigation menu and assign it to the primary menu slot in the theme:

1. Go to **Appearance | Menus**.

2. Click on **create a new menu** link and type in the name of your menu. I'm calling mine `navigation menu`.

3. Check the **Primary Menu** checkbox.

4. Drag the pages you want in your menu to the menu on the right and put them in the correct order. You can see my menu in the following screenshot:

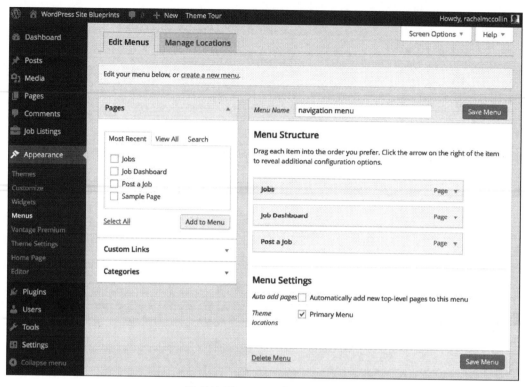

Fig 7.11: The menu admin screen

5. Now change the text in the link to the **Jobs** page. Click on the downwards arrow to the right of the **Jobs** menu item, delete the text in the **Navigation Label** field and type in Home, as shown in the following screenshot:

Fig 7.12: The menu admin screen with changes to the home page link

6. Click on the **Save Menu** button.

> If you're working with an existing site, you'll probably already have a menu set up. Just add the jobs pages to your existing menu.

In the **Menus** admin screen, my final saved menu looks like this:

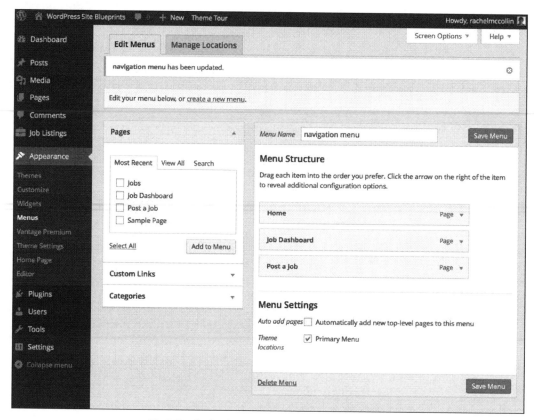

Fig 7.13: The final menu in the Menus admin screen

Configuring widgets

Now let's add some widgets to the theme's widget areas. I'm going to focus on the sidebar, but you can also add widgets to the footer. Follow these steps:

1. Go to **Appearance | Widgets**.
2. Drag the **Recent Jobs** widget to the **Sidebar** widget area. This widget is provided by the plugin and will automatically display the most recently added job listings:

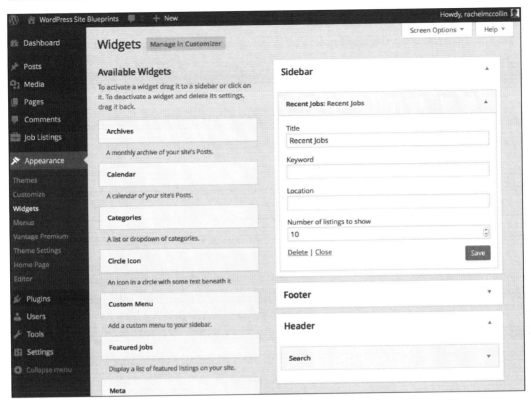

Fig 7.14: The Widgets admin screen

3. Click on the **Save** button for the widget.

So, that's the theme all set up! Now let's start adding some jobs.

Adding Job Listings

With the WP Job Manager plugin, you can add jobs in one of the two ways:

- As an administrator, adding them via the admin screens
- As an employer, posting jobs via the front end of the site

First, we'll add a job via the admin screens.

Adding a job via the admin screens

The administrator (that's you) will add jobs via the admin screens most of the time:

1. In the WordPress admin, go to **Job Listings | Add New**.

2. Add a title and description for the job and select the job categories and job types that apply to it (not that these are different from the categories you might be using for your site's posts, but just apply to jobs):

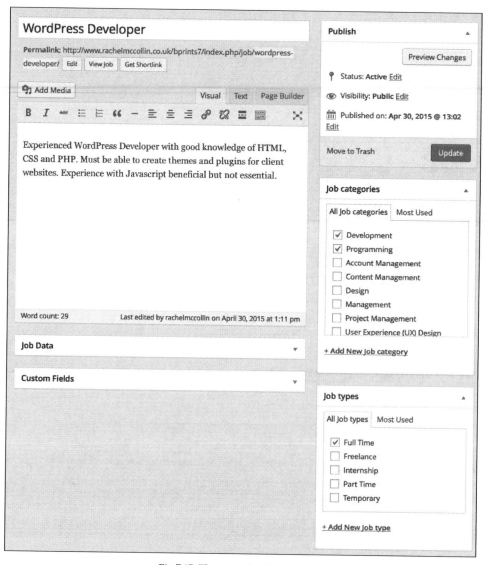

Fig 7.15: The new job admin screen

3. Scroll down to the **Job Data** metabox and add the following information:

   ○ **Location**: Enter your location here.

   ○ **Company Name** and **Company Tagline** if relevant.

   ○ **Company Logo**: Upload this using the media uploader, as shown in the following screenshot. Click on **Use file** to add it:

Fig 7.16: Uploading a company logo

   ○ **Position Filled**: Make sure this isn't checked.

○ **Listing Expiry Date**: Select the date the job listing expires using the date picker:

Fig 7.17: Picking an expiry date

○ **Application Email or URL**: Type in an e-mail address where applicants can mail their CV to or the URL of a page on a website where they can apply.

○ **Company Website**, **Company Twitter**, and **Company Video** if appropriate.

○ **Featured Listing**: Leave this unchecked for this job. If you want to highlight specific jobs on your board, you can use this to do so.

Your **Job Data** metabox will look similar to the following screenshot:

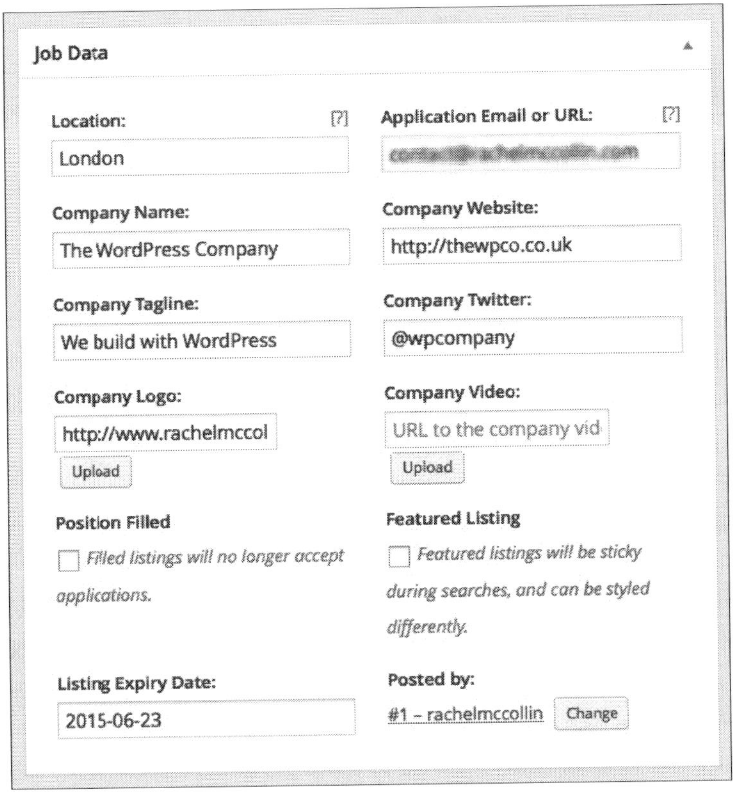

Fig 7.18: The completed Job Data metabox

4. Click on the **Publish** button to save and publish the listing.

Let's take a look at how this job looks on the site. Click on the **View Job** link to view it:

Fig 7.19: The job in the site's frontend

It looks good!

Now let's move on to adding a job via the frontend; this is how employers will do it.

Adding a job via the website

Although you can add jobs using the admin screens, employers won't have access to these. Instead, they have some specific screens that they can use to add and manage job listings. Follow these steps:

1. Open the website in your browser.
2. Click on the **Post a Job** link in the navigation menu.

3. Fill out the fields on the page to provide details of the job. You can see my example in the following screenshot:

Fig 7.20: The Post a Job page

4. Click on **Preview** to preview your job listing.

5. Check the preview and then click on **Edit listing** if you want to make changes or **Submit Listing** if you're happy with it. My preview is shown in the following screenshot:

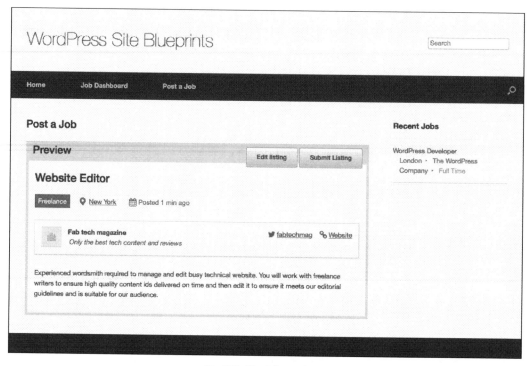

Fig 7.21: The job preview

Once you're happy with your listing and you've clicked on the **Submit Listing** button, it won't be posted to the site immediately. Instead, it will be held for moderation. Users will see a message letting them know this is happening.

Moderating and approving Job Listings

Once an employer posts a job, you'll need to moderate it before it's published. Let's check and publish that job we've just submitted:

1. In the WordPress admin, click on **Job Listings** and then on the **Pending** link above the listed jobs.

You'll see a list of all the pending jobs, as shown in the following screenshot:

Fig 7.22: The Job Listing moderation screen

2. Check the box next to all the jobs you want to approve and then select **Approve Jobs** from the **Bulk Actions** drop-down list, as shown in the following screenshot:

Fig 7.23: Approving jobs

3. Now click on the **Published** link to see all the published jobs, and the newly approved job will be included:

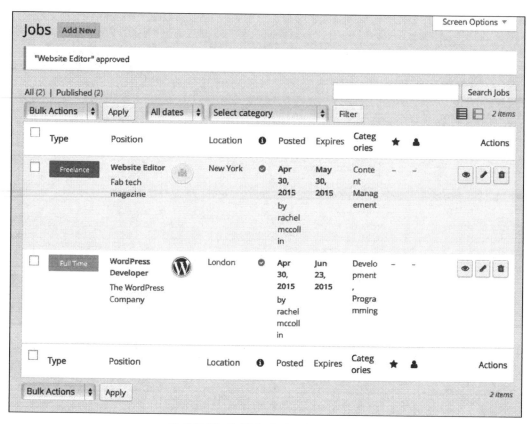

Fig 7.24: The Published jobs admin screen

4. Now try adding some more jobs either via the admin screens or the frontend. I've added some dummy jobs to my site and the jobs page now looks similar to this:

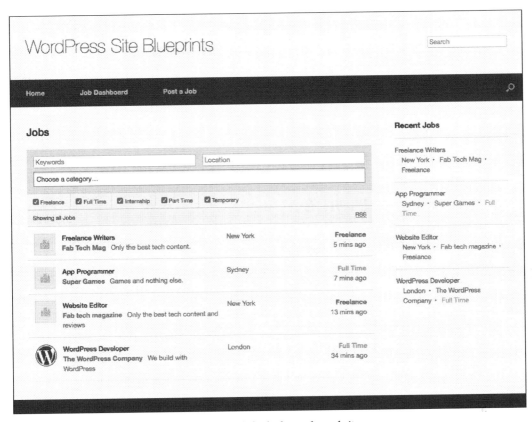

Fig 7.25: Published jobs on the website

Managing Job Listings

Once their job listings have been approved, employers can log in to your site and edit and manage them. They'll automatically receive an e-mail with their login details when they first create their account. This happens when they post their first job listing.

There are two options employers can use:

- They can mark jobs as filled, which means they'll no longer appear on the site (assuming you've configured the plugin to behave this way)
- They can edit the job details

Let's take a look at each of these.

Marking jobs as filled

To view the jobs they've posted, employers use the **Job Dashboard** page, as shown in the following screenshot:

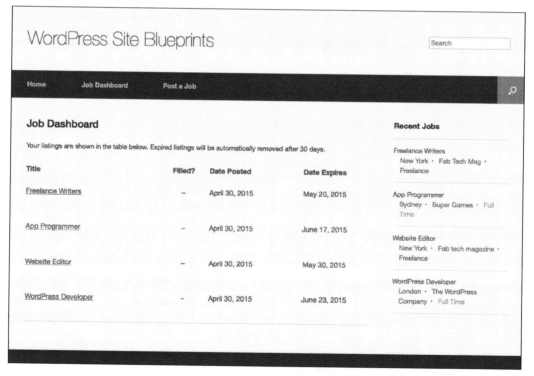

Fig 7.26: The Job Dashboard page

To mark jobs as filled, follow these steps:

1. On the main website, click on the **Job Dashboard** link in the main menu to go to the **Job Dashboard** screen.

2. Hover the mouse over the job you want to mark as filled.

3. Click on the **Mark filled** link.

4. The job listing will change in the dashboard to show that it's been filled:

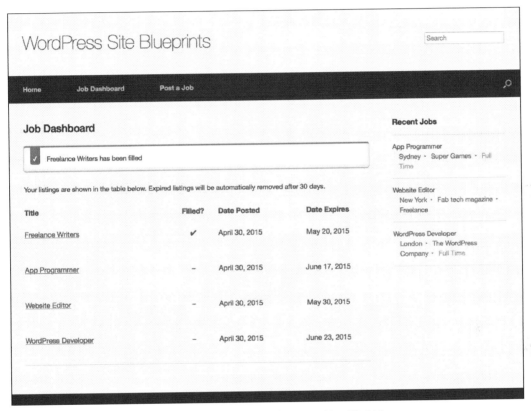

Fig 7.27: The Job Dashboard screen with a filled job

If you visit the main jobs page, you'll find that the job is no longer displayed.

Editing jobs

Employers can also edit jobs they've posted by following these steps:

1. On the main website, click on the **Job Dashboard** link in the main menu to go to the **Job Dashboard** screen.

2. Hover the mouse over the job you want to edit.

3. Click on the **Edit** link to display the editing fields, as shown in the following screenshot:

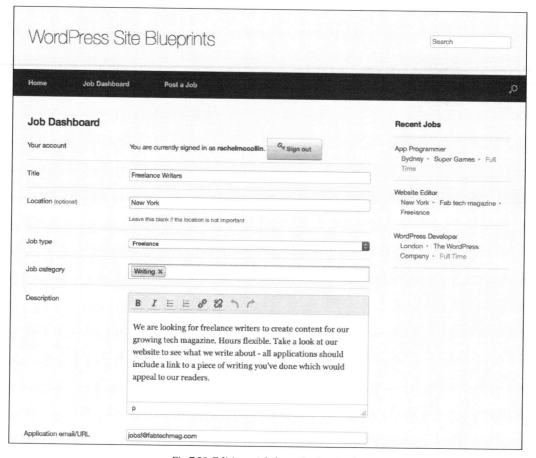

Fig 7.28: Editing a job from the frontend

4. Make your changes and click on the **Save changes** button.

Searching and applying for jobs

Since you've added job categories and job types to your jobs, people can use these (along with keywords) to search for jobs.

For example, the following screenshot shows a search for full time, part time, or temporary jobs with the **developer** keyword:

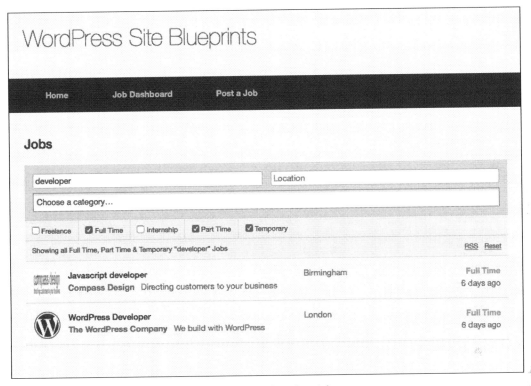

Fig 7.29: Searching for a job

To view the job details, users click on the job title to view its page on your site, as shown in the following screenshot:

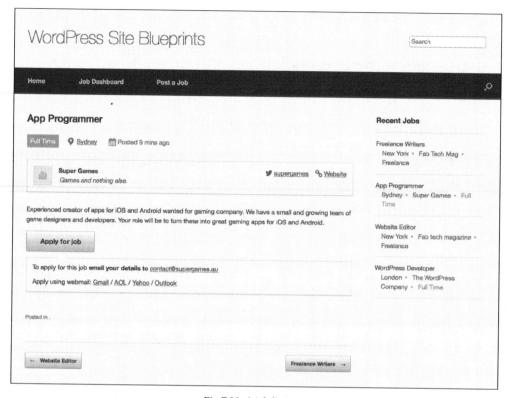

Fig 7.30: A job listing

To apply for the job, they click on the **Apply for job** button. This will do one of two things:

- If the employer has provided an e-mail address for applications, it will open up their e-mail program so that they can send an e-mail with their CV and application.

- If the employer has provided a URL (maybe to the job listing on their own site), it will display a link for the user to click on, as shown in the following screenshot:

Fig 7.31: Applying for a job

Managing users

Each employer who posts jobs on your site will be given a user account, which they can use to log in and manage their job listings. They are given the employer user role, which is an extra role created by the plugin.

As the administrator, you can manage these accounts by editing their details, changing passwords, and deleting them if need be.

You can access all of your users via the main **Users** screen in the WordPress admin. The following screenshot shows my **Users** admin screen with one employer signed up:

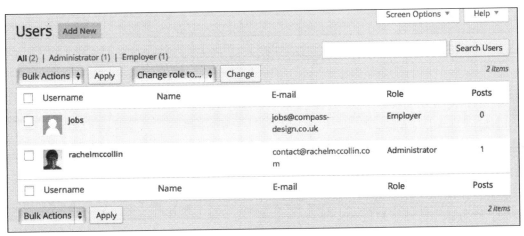

Fig 7.32: Managing users

Summary

A jobs board can be a really useful resource for your business or your community. It can be a standalone resource or an added extra in a blog or community site, or maybe something you can use on your own business site to recruit staff

In this chapter, you learned how to use the WP Job Manager plugin to create your own jobs board. You installed and configured the plugin and also a suitable theme. You added jobs both via the WordPress admin and the website. You moderated and published jobs submitted via your site. You also learned how to manage job listings and edit them, search and apply for jobs, and manage the users, who will be the employers posting jobs, on your site.

Well done, you've created your first jobs board. Good luck with your recruitment!

8

Creating a Team
Communications Site

If you want to find a way to communicate with other members of a team without using a public tool such as Facebook and LinkedIn or an expensive project management solution such as Basecamp, the good news is that WordPress can help.

It's easy to set up a private WordPress site that you and your colleagues can use to keep up to date and discuss ideas and progress, and to configure that site so that people are notified when their updates are commented on.

In this chapter, I'll show you how to do this. You'll learn how to:

- Use the P2 theme to create a team site
- Configure and customize the P2 theme
- Add widgets to your site to make it more user-friendly
- Configure discussion and reading settings to make your site work for the team
- Add team members to your site and use a plugin to display links to their updates on the site
- Install a plugin to make your site private so that only logged in members can view it

The P2 theme was created by the WordPress core team to speed up its own internal communication. It's designed specifically for this purpose and is constantly being improved and updated. So it's a good choice for your site!

Let's get started!

Installing and configuring the P2 theme

The first step is to install the P2 theme in a fresh WordPress installation. If you're not sure how to install WordPress, take a look at *Chapter 1, Migrating a Static Site to WordPress.*

Installing the theme

Perform the following steps to install a theme:

1. In the WordPress admin, go to **Appearance | Themes**.
2. Click on the **Add New** button.
3. In the search box, type P2.

   WordPress will display all the themes matching your search terms, as shown in the following screenshot:

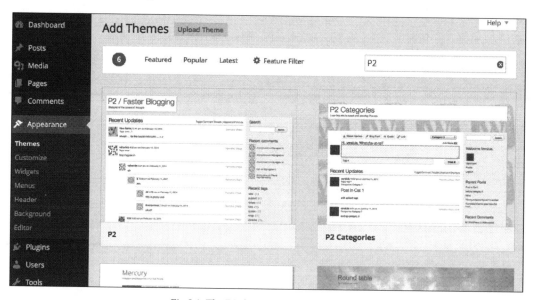

Fig 8.1: The P2 theme installation process

4. Select **P2** and click on the **Install** button.
5. Once the theme has been installed, click on the **Activate** button.

The theme will now be active.

Now, if you visit your site's front page, it will look similar to the following screenshot:

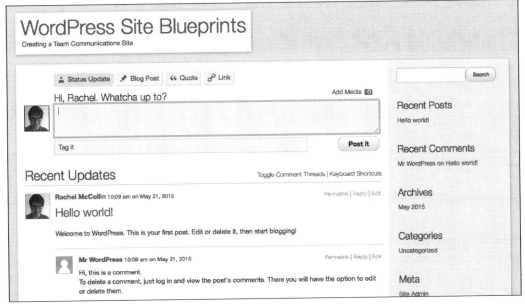

Fig 8.2: The site's home page with P2 activated

Now that the theme is installed, let's do some configuration.

Configuring the P2 options

P2 comes with some options you can configure. Perform the following steps to configure the P2 options:

1. If you haven't already configured the options, go back to the admin screens.

2. Go to **Appearance | Theme Options**.

3. Edit the P2 options screen as follows:

    ○ **Posting Access**: Check this box to allow all the subscribers to post to the site.

    ○ **Hide Threads**: Uncheck this box so that people can see comment threads.

    ○ **Custom Background Color**: Select a color for your site's background or select a background image from the radio buttons next to **Background Image** if you like (warning: they're a bit ugly!).

    ○ **Sidebar display**: Uncheck this box so that the recent activities can be seen in the sidebar.

- ○ **Post prompt**: Leave this as it is or write your own prompt. I've typed `Update the team here:`.

- ○ **Post Titles**: Check this box. **Post Titles** makes it easier to scan posts and see what you need to read.

Your options screen will look similar to the following screenshot:

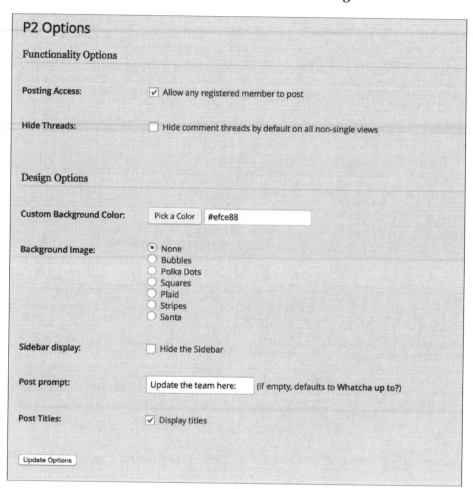

Fig 8.3: The P2 options screen

4. Scroll down and click on the **Update Options** button.

Adding widgets

Next, let's add some widgets to the theme's sidebar:

1. Go to **Appearance | Widgets**.

2. Delete the default widgets that are in the **Sidebar** widget area.

3. Add the following widgets:

    ○ **Recent Posts**

    ○ **P2 Recent Comments**

    ○ **P2 Recent Tags**

    ○ **Meta**

    If you want, you can change the titles of the first three widgets and you can change the number of posts, comments, or tags displayed.

4. Save each of them. Your **Sidebar** widget area should look similar to the following screenshot:

Fig 8.4: The Widgets screen with widgets added

Now your home page will look a bit different:

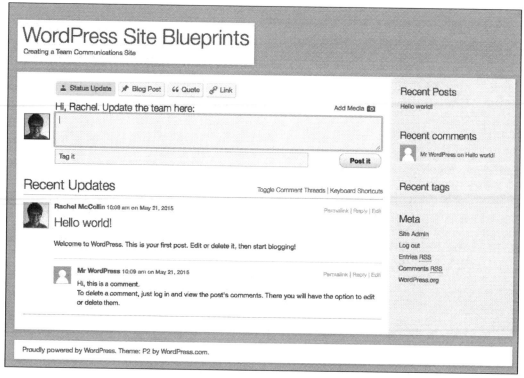

Fig 8.5: The home page with customizations and widgets

Now that you've got the theme installed and configured, let's move on to adding some users.

Adding users to your site

A team site will only be useful if team members are added to it. You can let people register themselves as users on the site using the WordPress registration screen, but we will not do this here. Later, in this chapter, we'll install a plugin that prevents anyone without an account on the site from viewing it, which means the administrator (that's you!) needs to add each user to the site.

Adding users

Follow these steps to add users to your site:

1. In the WordPress admin, go to **Users** | **Add New**.

2. Add your first user's details. If you don't have any users yet, add a dummy user, as I've done in the following screenshot:

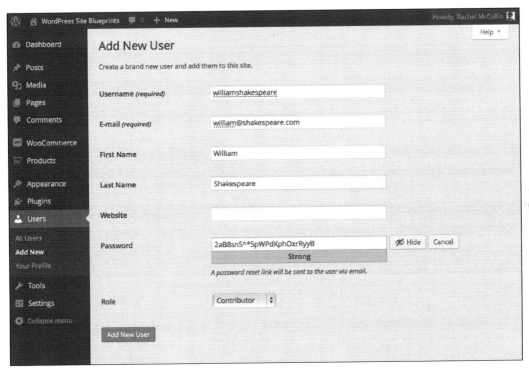

Fig 8.6: Adding a new user

3. Make sure your user has the **Contributor** role so that they can add posts.

4. Click on the **Add New User** button to add the new user.

5. Repeat this with all of your users. As you can see in the following screenshot, I've added a few more dummy users, and my team is turning out to be quite literary:

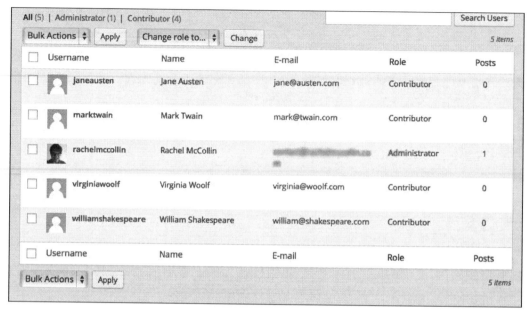

Fig 8.7: New users on the Users screen

Listing users in the sidebar

Now that you have some users, it's useful to be able to display them on your site's frontend. We're going to install a plugin called **Author Avatars List**, which displays the avatar for each user along with a link to their author page. This means that anyone using the site can quickly find everything posted by an individual user.

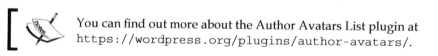 You can find out more about the Author Avatars List plugin at https://wordpress.org/plugins/author-avatars/.

So let's start by installing the plugin.

1. In the WordPress admin, go to **Plugins | Add New**.

2. In the search box, type `Author Avatars List`.

3. From the plugins that WordPress selected for you, select the **Author Avatars List** plugin and click on the **Install Now** button.

4. When the plugin is installed, click on the **Activate** link.

Now that the plugin is installed and activated, you have access to a widget. Let's add that to the sidebar:

1. Go to **Appearance | Widgets**.

2. Drag the **Author Avatars** widget to the **Sidebar** widget area, placing it below the other widgets.

3. Configure the widget settings in the **Basic** section as follows:
    - **Title**: Type `Team Members`
    - **Show roles**: Check **Administrator, Editor, Author**, and **Contributor**
    - **Link users to**: Select **Author Page**
    - **Display options**: Check **Show name, Show number of posts**, and **Show link to authors last post**
    - **Avatar size**: Type `200`

4. Now scroll down to the **Advanced** section and add these configurations:
    - **Sorting order**: Select **Last Name**
    - **Sorting direction**: Select **Ascending**
    - Leave the rest of the fields blank

5. Click on **Save** to save your settings. Your widget settings will look similar to the following screenshot:

Fig 8.8: The Author Avatars widget settings

Now if you look at the sidebar on your site's frontend, it will contain the author avatars, names, and post links:

Fig 8.9: Author avatars in the sidebar

At the moment, my avatars are displaying a placeholder image because I've used dummy e-mail addresses. If you want to add avatars for your users, you can either do this by setting up an avatar for them at `http://gravatar.com` or by using an avatar upload plugin such as WP User Avatar (`https://wordpress.org/plugins/wp-user-avatar/`).

Configuring privacy and discussions

As this site is just for your team to use, you'll want to make it private so that only logged in users can access it. You'll also need to make some changes to the discussion settings so that logged in members can add comments.

Hiding the site from search engines

First, let's make sure that the site doesn't get picked up by search engines:

1. Go to **Settings | Reading**.
2. Check the **Search Engine Visibility** box, as shown in the following screenshot:

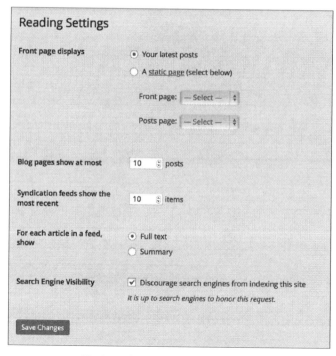

Fig 8.10: The Reading Settings screen

3. Click on the **Save Changes** button.

Now search engines will be discouraged from finding your site; this makes it less likely that people who shouldn't have access to your site will stumble upon it.

Configuring Discussion Settings

Now let's configure the discussion settings for the site. Follow these steps:

1. Go to **Settings | Discussion**.

2. On the **Discussion Settings** screen, check the following settings:

    ° **Allow people to post comments on new articles**

    ° **Users must be registered and logged in to comment**

    ° **Enable threaded comments 5 levels deep**

3. **Make sure the rest of the options are unchecked**

4. Scroll down and click on the **Save Changes** button.

Your **Discussion Settings** screen will look similar to the following screenshot:

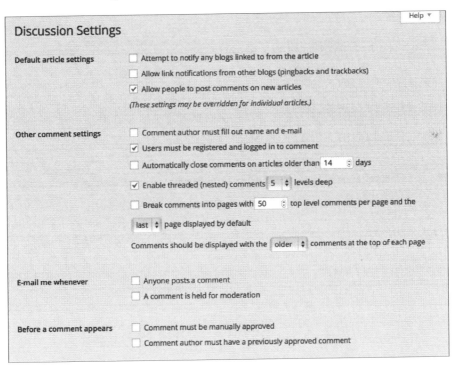

Fig 8.11: Discussion settings

This means that your site won't use pingbacks or trackbacks (these notify you when another site links to your site, which won't be happening here as this is a private site), and comments will only be open to logged in users. You don't need to moderate their comments as they're members of your team and you want to enable easy commenting and posting for them.

Notifying post authors of comments

By default, when someone posts a comment in reply to one of the posts on your site, both the post author and the administrator will be notified. As this site will have a lot of comments posted to it and you know there's no risk of spam, you, as the administrator, don't need to be notified of every new comment.

So let's install a plugin that fixes that. The **Comment Moderation E-mail only to Author** plugin (`https://wordpress.org/plugins/comment-moderation-e-mail-to-post-author/`) prevents e-mails being sent to the administrator every time a comment is posted, but ensures that post authors will still be notified. Follow these steps:

1. Go to **Plugins | Add New**.
2. In the search box, type `Comment Moderation`.
3. From the plugins that WordPress selected for you, select the **Comment Moderation E-mail only to Author** plugin and click on the **Install Now** button.
4. When the plugin is installed, click on the **Activate** link.

That's all you need to do; simply by activating the plugin, you'll prevent e-mails going to the administrator unless the administrator is also the post author.

Limiting access to your site

The next step is to limit access to the site so that only the users with an account can see it. To do this, you simply install the **Force Login** plugin (which you can find at `https://wordpress.org/plugins/wp-force-login/`). Note that this is one of many plugins available that does this job, and in a corporate environment, you may need a specific plugin that works with your internal systems. This is the plugin I like to use with simple sites like this one, however. Perform these steps:

1. Go to **Plugins | Add New**.
2. In the search box, type `Force Login`.

3. From the plugins that WordPress selected for you, select the **Force Login** plugin and click on the **Install Now** button.

4. When the plugin is installed, click on the **Activate** link.

You don't need to do anything else to configure the plugin. The following screenshot shows that it's activated on your site:

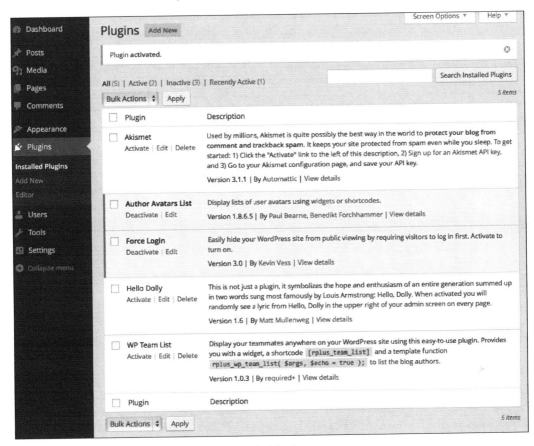

Fig 8.12: The Plugins screen

Now if you log out of your site and try to access it, you'll have to log in first, as shown in the following screenshot:

Fig 8.13: Forced login

Adding posts and comments to the site

Now that your site is set up and you've added users, all they need to do to add a new post is log in and start typing:

- To add a new post (or update), type in the box at the top of the screen. Type or select tags below the textbox and click on the **Post it** button.
- You can add different styles of post (or post formats) by clicking one of the buttons above the textbox before typing in your text:
    - ° Selecting **Blog Post** means you can add a title to your post

○ Selecting **Quote** means you can add a quote and citation

○ Selecting **Link** means you can add a link without any other text

- To reply to a post, simply click on the **Reply** link next to the post and type your response.

Whenever someone replies to a post, the post author will receive an e-mail notifying them, meaning they can reply back if they want.

The P2 theme formats the different types of post differently. The following screenshot shows how my site looks with a quote, a blog post, a link, and some updates with replies added:

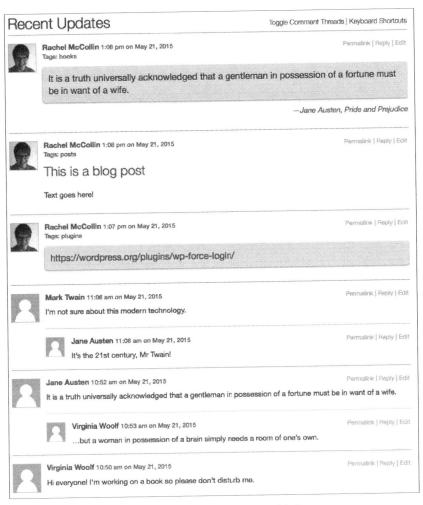

Fig 8.14: The site with content added

Summary

WordPress is a great tool for creating a private site for your team to communicate with each other. In this chapter, you learned how to do this using the P2 theme.

You installed and configured the theme and then you used plugins to provide an author listing widget, make the site private, and alter comment notifications. You also configured the reading and discussion settings to prevent search engines from crawling the site and allow logged in users to post comments without moderation.

Now all you need to do is to add all your team members to your site and start using it. Enjoy!

9
Creating a Gallery Site

If you're a keen photographer, you'll want to show your work off online. Whether you're an enthusiastic amateur, a professional needing a portfolio site, or you've been hired by a photographer to build a site for them, WordPress makes it easy to create a gallery site and show your images to the world.

In this chapter, we'll see how to use the most popular free WordPress gallery plugin out there—NextGEN Gallery. Here's what you'll do:

- Install a theme for your gallery site
- Install the NextGEN Gallery plugin, which adds more flexibility than what's provided by WordPress' built-in galleries
- Create some galleries
- Create some posts to place your galleries in
- Edit images in your gallery right in WordPress—no image editing software is required
- Create an album with multiple galleries in it and use a page to display that
- Add your galleries to your site's menu and widgets

So let's get started!

Installing a theme

The first step is to install a theme for your gallery site. I'm going to work with a clean WordPress installation. If you're adding a gallery to an existing site with a theme installed, you can skip this step and move straight on to installing the plugin.

I'm assuming you've already got WordPress installed. If you need help with doing this, refer to *Chapter 1, Migrating a Static Site to WordPress*.

Let's install the Baskerville theme:

1. Go to **Appearance | Themes**.
2. Click on the **Add New** button.
3. In the **Search** box, type `Baskerville`.
4. WordPress will find the Baskerville theme for you. Click on **Install**.
5. Once the theme has been installed, click on the **Activate** link.

The Baskerville theme will now be active on your site:

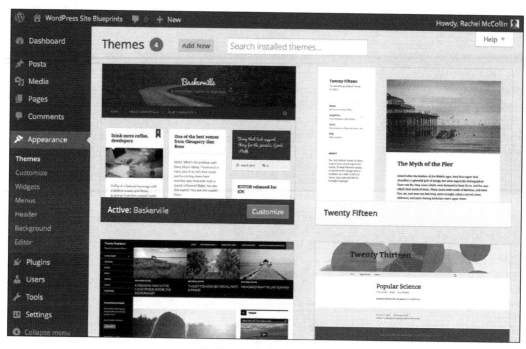

Fig 9.1: The installed theme

Now let's customize the theme by adding a header image. Baskerville includes space for an image that's 1,440px wide and 221px tall on its home page. You can either upload an image that you've already cropped to these dimensions or crop it after uploading it. If you go for the second option, make sure your image is at least 1,440px wide. Follow these steps:

1. Go to **Appearance | Customize**.
2. Click on **Header Image** on the left-hand side of the screen.
3. Click on the **Add new image** button.
4. When prompted, upload your image. Crop it if you need to.

Your image will now be displayed in the theme customizer:

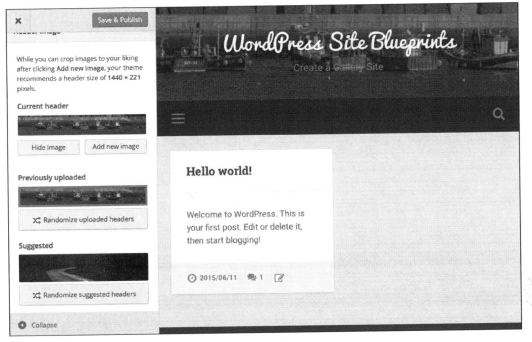

Fig 9.2: The customized theme

I've uploaded a photo that I'll also be including in one of my galleries. Next, you need to add some galleries, but to do this, you need to install the plugin.

Installing the NextGEN Gallery plugin

Before you can add any galleries, you'll need to install the plugin by performing these steps:

1. Go to **Plugins** | **Add New**.
2. In the search box, type NextGEN.
3. WordPress will display the plugin. Click on the **Install Now** button.
4. Once the plugin has been installed, click on the **Activate** link.

You'll now find that a **Gallery** item is added to your admin menu, with a number of subitems you can use to create and manage galleries and albums.

Let's use one of these to add some galleries.

Adding galleries

One of the great things about this plugin is that it lets you upload your images and then manipulate them in WordPress. It also lets you upload larger images than you're able to via the standard media uploader; this means you don't have to crop them before uploading. You can dive straight into uploading your images and creating your gallery:

1. In the WordPress admin, go to **Gallery | Add Gallery / Images**.
2. Click on **Create a new gallery** in the drop-down menu at the top of the screen and type the name of the gallery in the field next to it.
3. Click on the **Add Files** button and select the files you want to upload.
4. After selecting all your files, click on the **Start Upload** button.

   The plugin will upload all of your images for you and display them on the screen:

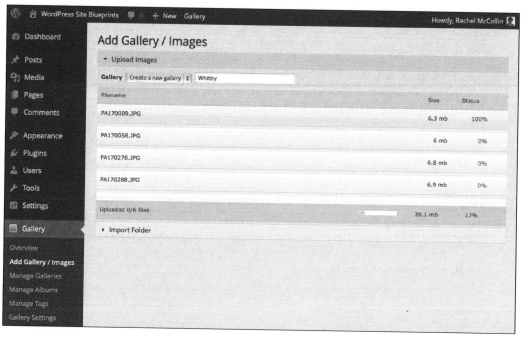

Fig 9.3: The gallery with images uploaded

5. Now repeat this a few times so that you have more than one gallery. I've added some photos I've taken on photography trips, and have created three galleries. You can see all your galleries if you go to **Gallery | Overview**:

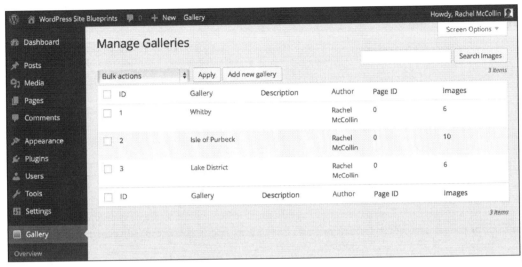

Fig 9.4: The gallery overview screen with the three galleries added

Now that you've added your galleries, you need to display them somewhere. You can use posts or pages to do this; for a photo blog, posts display best with this theme, so that's what we'll use.

Creating posts to display galleries

Now you need to create posts to hold your galleries.

Adding a gallery to a post

Displaying a gallery within a post is really easy; the plugin adds a button to the post editor to help you. To add a gallery, perform the following steps:

1. To create a new post, go to **Posts | Add New**.

2. Give your post the same name as the gallery you'll be displaying it in (or a related name; it's up to you!).

3. Click on the green box above the content pane. When you hover your mouse over it you'll see the words **Attach NextGEN Gallery to Post**.

4. The **NextGEN Gallery** dialog box will appear. Start by clicking on the **Select a display type** section if it isn't already open:

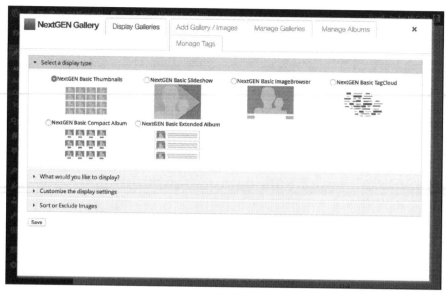

Fig 9.5: The NextGEN Gallery dialog box's display type section

5. Select **NextGEN Basic Thumbnails**.

6. Now click on the **What would you like to display?** section:

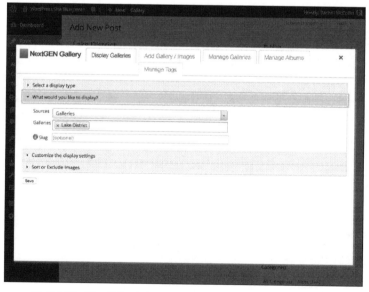

Fig 9.6: The NextGEN Gallery dialog box's what to display section

7. In the **Sources** drop-down menu, select **Galleries**.

8. In the **Galleries** field, start typing the name of the gallery you want to insert or click on it when the gallery names appear.

9. Now click on the **Customize the display settings** section:

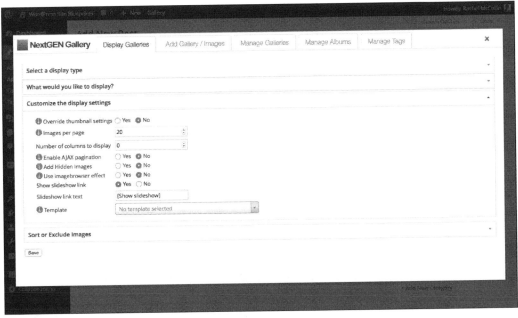

Fig 9.7: The NextGEN Gallery dialog box's display settings section

10. Leave the defaults as they are because they fit nicely with our theme. If you're using your own theme, you might want to change them, for example, changing the maximum dimensions.

11. The next section is the **Sort or Exclude Images** section:

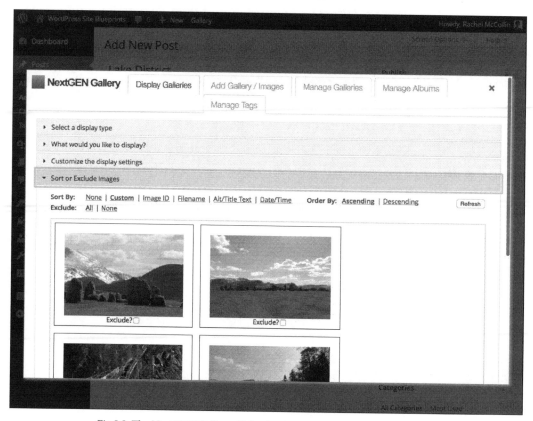

Fig 9.8: The NextGEN Gallery dialog box's Sort or Exclude Images section

12. If you want to change the order of the images in your gallery, drag them into place.

13. Finally, click on the **Save** button.

A thumbnail image for the gallery will be displayed in your editing screen.

Adding a featured image from your gallery

For an image from the gallery to be displayed on the site's main page, we need to add a featured image next. This is because the Baskerville theme displays featured images prominently. If your theme doesn't, you may not need to do this (although I recommend using a theme that supports and displays featured images as it will really enhance your gallery site). Follow these steps:

1. Still in the post editing screen, scroll down and click on the **Set NextGEN featured image** link in the **Featured Image** metabox.

2. In the dialog box that appears, select the gallery you want to choose an image from and its images will be displayed:

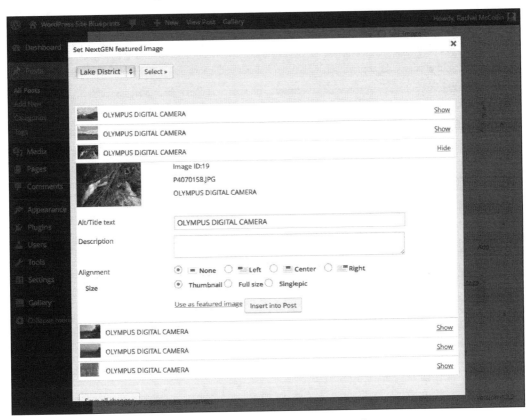

Fig 9.9: Selecting a featured image from a gallery

3. Select the image you want. Click on the **Use as featured image** link and close the dialog box. Now, click on the **Publish** button to save your post.

Don't forget to add alt and title text to your images. It will make your site accessible to people using screen readers and will also help with your search engine rankings. Use descriptive text for these.

Here's how my post looks on the frontend of the site; you can see the featured image at the top and the thumbnails at the bottom:

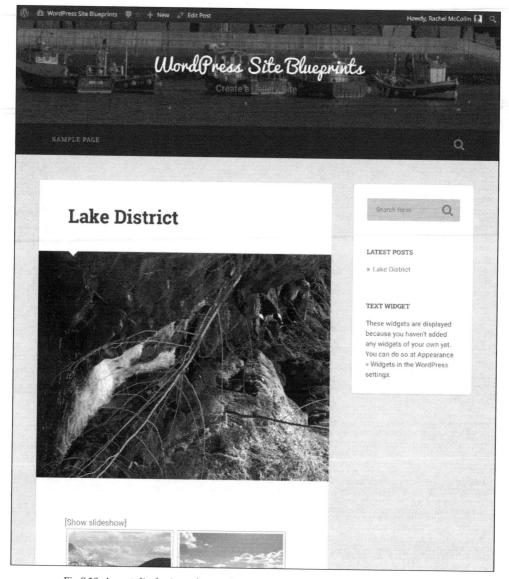

Fig 9.10: A post displaying a featured image and gallery on the frontend of the site

If I scroll down, you can see all my thumbnails displayed:

Fig 9.11: A post displaying a gallery on the frontend of the site

You might have spotted that one of these images has been rotated by 90 degrees (the one at the bottom right). We'll fix that a bit later on when we come to editing images.

Now repeat this process for your other galleries. Create the same number of posts as you have galleries, and give each of them the same name as the gallery you'll use the post to display. Add a gallery and featured image to each post in the same way as you did for the first.

Here are all of my posts in the post listing admin screen:

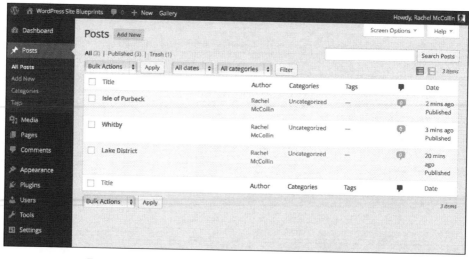

Fig 9.12: Three posts for three galleries—the Posts admin screen

As the Baskerville theme uses a featured image on the main blog page, you can also see images on my site's home page:

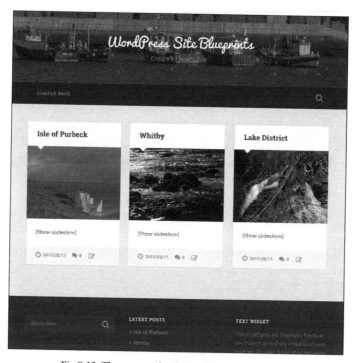

Fig 9-13: Three posts for three galleries—frontend

Now let's edit a couple of images, including the one that's rotated by 90 degrees.

Editing images

One of the most useful features of the NextGEN Gallery plugin is the fact that it lets you edit your images from the WordPress admin. This is great if you don't have an image editing program you can use or if you spot something you want to change after uploading your images (as we have!).

Rotating images

Let's use the image editing capabilities to rotate that image and resize its thumbnail:

1. Back in the WordPress admin screens, go to **Gallery | Manage Galleries** to view the **Manage Galleries** screen:

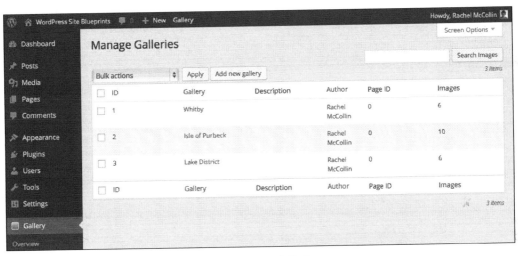

Fig 9.14: The Manage Galleries screen

2. Click on the gallery that contains the image you want to edit. In my case it's **Lake District**.

3.   The gallery editing screen will be displayed:

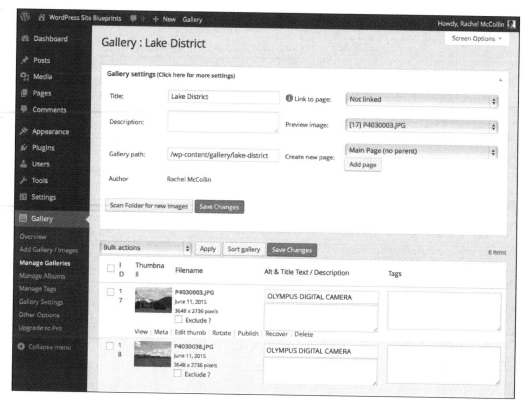

Fig 9.15: The gallery editing screen

4. Scroll down until you can see the image you want to manipulate:

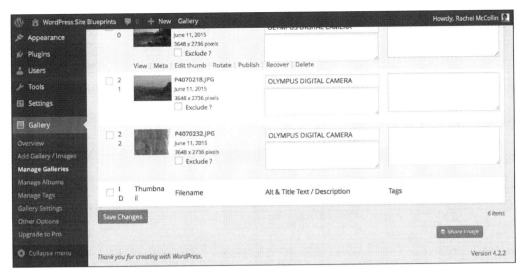

Fig 9.16: The gallery editing screen—image to be manipulated

5. Hover over the image with your mouse and click on the **Rotate** link.

6. The image will be deployed in a dialog box. Select the correct checkbox to rotate the image so that it's upright. In my case it's **90° counter-clockwise**:

Fig 9.17: Rotating an image

The image will be displayed the right way up:

Fig 9.18: The corrected image

7. Click on the **Update** button to save your changes.

Cropping thumbnails

The next step is to edit the thumbnail (as you've rotated the image, the thumbnail will default to the very top of the image, which doesn't show much detail):

1. Still in the gallery editing screen, hover over the same image and click on the **Edit thumb** link.

2. A dialog box will appear where you can crop the image to the correct size for its thumbnail. Crop the image so that it looks great as a thumbnail:

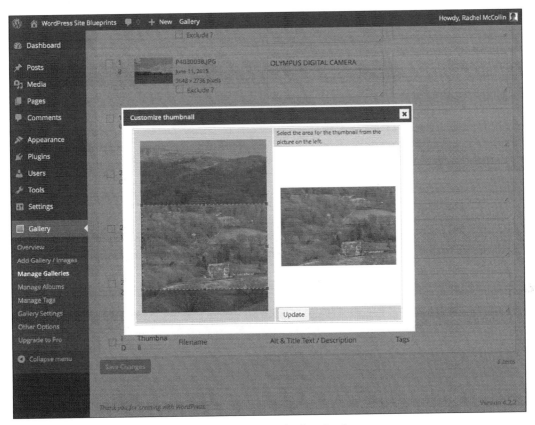

Fig 9.19: Cropping the thumbnail

3. Click on the **Update** button to save your changes.

4. Finally, back in the gallery editing screen, click on the **Save Changes** button to save what you've done.

You'll now find that when you view your gallery on the frontend, the image will be the right way up and the thumbnail crop will be correct:

Fig 9.20: The corrected image on the frontend

Now that we've added galleries and edited an image, let's move on to creating albums.

Creating an album

With the NextGEN Gallery plugin, an album is a group of galleries that you display together on one page. You can include a gallery in more than one album and each album can include multiple galleries. It's not far off categories in WordPress posts.

Here, we'll create a gallery to contain our three albums and then create a page to display the album.

Creating the album using the NextGEN Gallery plugin

Creating an album is done via the NextGEN Gallery screens. Follow these steps:

1. In the WordPress admin, select **Gallery | Manage Albums**.

    This will display the **Manage Albums** screen:

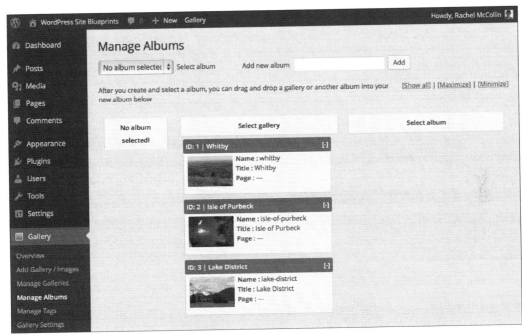

Fig 9.21: The Manage Albums screen with no albums

2. In the **Add new album** field, type the name of your album. I'm calling mine `Landscape Photography`.

3. Click on the **Add** button.

4. Now drag the galleries you want to display into your new album, as shown in the following screenshot:

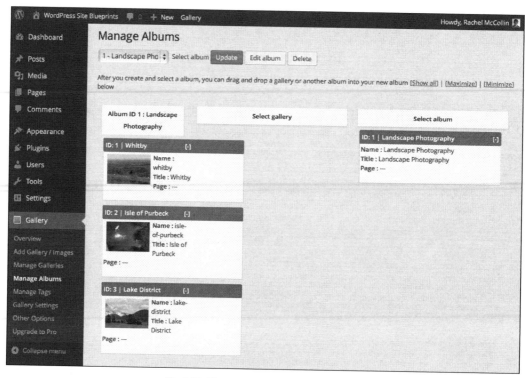

Fig 9.22: The galleries added to my album

5. Once you're happy that you've added the right galleries, click on the **Update** button to save your changes.

Now you need to display your album somewhere. Let's create a page.

Displaying an album in a page

The first step is to create a page and then we'll add the album to it. Follow these steps:

1. Go to **Pages | Add New** to create your new page.

2. Give your page a name.

3. Above the content pane, click on the green box that you used to add a gallery previously.

4. Click on the **What would you like to display?** section:

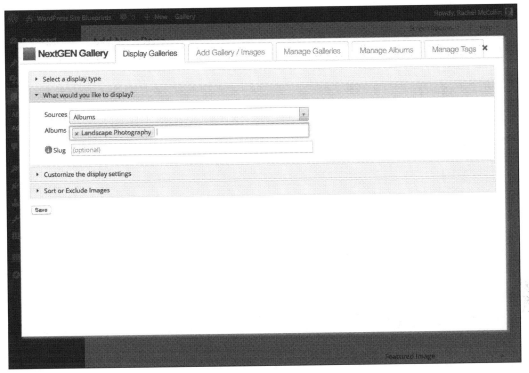

Fig 9.23: Adding a gallery to a page— the What would you like to display section

5. In the **Sources** drop-down menu, select **Albums**.

6. In the **Albums** field, start typing the name of your album and select the album's name when it appears.

7. Click on the **Select a display type** section.

8. Select **NextGEN Basic Compact Album**.

9. Click on the **Save** button.

A thumbnail image will be added to your page on the admin screen:

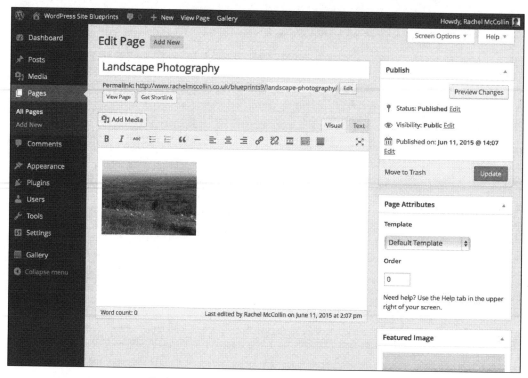

Fig 9.24: Page editing screen with an album added

10. Now add a featured image from a gallery in the same way as you did in your posts and click on the **Publish** button to save and publish your page.

Your page will display the featured image and the three galleries on the frontend:

Fig 9.25: The page with an album on the frontend

If a visitor clicks on one of these galleries, they'll be able to view the individual gallery.

Adding a menu and widgets

Now that we have all our images in place, we need to make it easier for visitors to find them. We can do this by adding a menu and some widgets.

Adding a menu

Let's start by adding a navigation menu:

1. In the WordPress admin, go to **Appearance | Menus**.

2. If your site doesn't already have a menu set up, click on the **create a new menu** link.

3. Type the menu's name in the **Menu Name** field.

4. Create a custom link for your home page (which will be the site's main URL) and drag the page you've just created into the menu along with that:

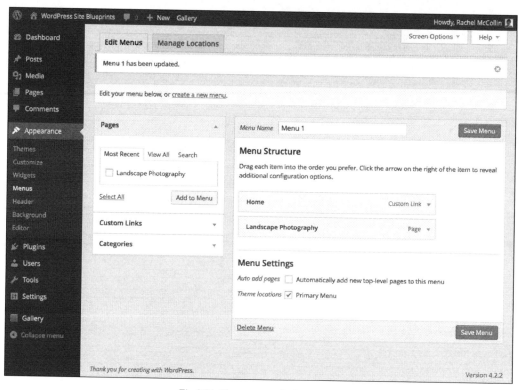

Fig 9.26: The menus admin screen

5. Check the **Primary Menu** checkbox to ensure your menu appears in the theme.

6. Click on the **Save Menu** button to save your changes.

Adding widgets

Next, let's add some widgets to the sidebar and footer:

1. Go to **Appearance | Widgets**.

2. Add the **Search** widget to the **Footer A** widget area (assuming you're using the Baskerville theme which has this widget area). Click on the **Save** button for the widget.

3. Add the **Recent Posts** widget to the **Footer B** widget area. Give it the title `Latest Galleries`, as shown in the following screenshot:

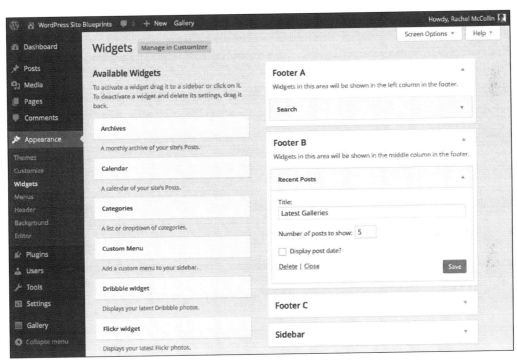

Fig 9.27: The Latest Galleries widget

4. Click on **Save**.

5. Add **NextGEN Widget** to the **Footer C** widget area, as shown in the following screenshot:

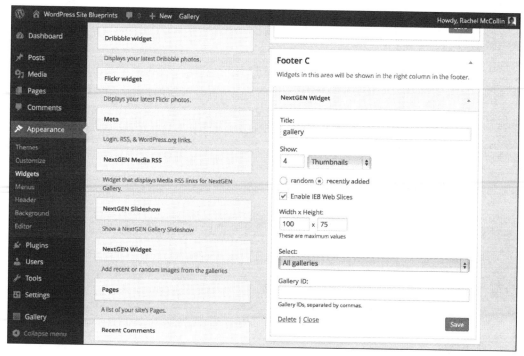

Fig 9.28: The NextGEN Gallery widget

6. Edit the settings as follows:
    - **Title**: gallery
    - Show four thumbnails
    - Check **Enable IE8 Web Slices**
    - **Width x Height**: 100 **x** 75
    - **Select**: **All galleries**

7. Click on the **Save** button.

8. Next, add the **Text** widget to the **Sidebar** widget area and add some text about your gallery site, as shown in the following screenshot. You can add a lot more detail than I have if you like!

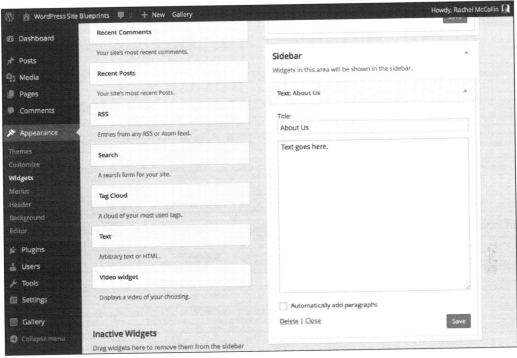

Fig 9.29: The Text widget

9. Click on the **Save** button for this widget.

 If you're using a different theme with different widget areas, add these widgets to the widget areas available to you.

Here's how the footer looks now:

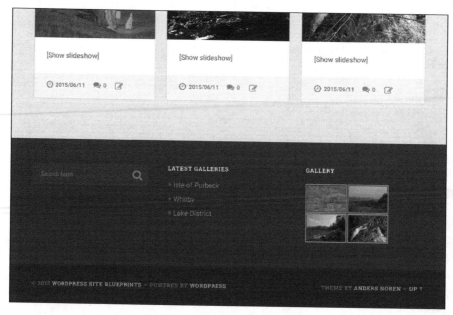

Fig 9.30: The footer with the widgets

The following screenshot shows the sidebar with a **Text** widget:

Fig 9.31: The sidebar with a Text widget

Now that you have your widgets and menu in place, the site feels a lot more polished and easier to navigate through.

Summary

WordPress is a great tool for creating a gallery site and showcasing your photographs. You can use the default galleries that come with WordPress, but with the addition of a great free plugin such as NextGEN Gallery, you can take things a bit further.

In this chapter, you learned how to install a theme for your gallery site and the NextGEN plugin. You then created some galleries and added them to posts along with featured images, edited images in your gallery, and created an album with some galleries in it and added that to a page. Finally, you added a menu and some widgets to help people navigate around your site.

Good job! In the next and final chapter, you'll learn how to create a membership site.

10
Creating a Membership Site

WordPress comes with some great membership features out of the box. You can create accounts for your users, require them to log in to access content, manage multiple users, and more. But with the addition of a free plugin, you can create a fully-featured membership site and make money from it.

In this chapter, we'll build a membership site using the **Paid Memberships Pro** plugin. The site will include different tiers of membership with different price levels. It will require people to subscribe and log in to access specific content and will link to PayPal so that you can take payments easily.

Designing and planning your membership site

Before you start building your site, it's a good idea to identify exactly what you want it to do. For example:

- Will all content be restricted to members or will some be available to all?
- Will you charge for membership?
- Will you have different membership levels with different content?
- Will your site include advertising (maybe with no advertising for members)?
- Will you offer free membership?
- What will you do to communicate with your members? Will you send them notifications of new content?

- Will you use the data you have about your members to sell products? Make sure you have permission from your members if you do this.

- Will you let your members talk to each other? You might want to think about installing BuddyPress if you want an interactive membership site; if it is the case, refer to *Chapter 2, Creating a Social Media Site*.

Once you've identified how you want your membership site to work, you'll be able to find a plugin with the features that you need. In this chapter, I'll be using the Paid Memberships Pro plugin (`http://www.paidmembershipspro.com/demo/`), which is free on the WordPress plugin repository and lets you create multiple membership levels with different subscriptions. It also lets you hook up to PayPal and creates pages for signing up and logging in.

Our site won't include advertising, but if you want to do so, you might want to check out a guide to adding Google Adsense at `http://www.wpbeginner.com/beginners-guide/how-to-add-google-adsense-to-your-wordpress-site/` or look at WPMU DEV's premium membership plugin (which includes advertising options) at `https://premium.wpmudev.org/project/membership/`.

So let's start by installing the plugin!

Installing the Paid Memberships Pro plugin

The first thing to do is to install the Paid Memberships Pro plugin. Note that I'm using the default Twenty Fifteen theme on my site, so I won't be installing another theme. If you'd rather pick a different theme or use your own, you can do so. Follow these steps:

1. In the WordPress admin, go to **Plugins** | **Add New**.
2. In the search box, type `Paid Memberships Pro`.

The Paid Memberships Pro plugin will be shown:

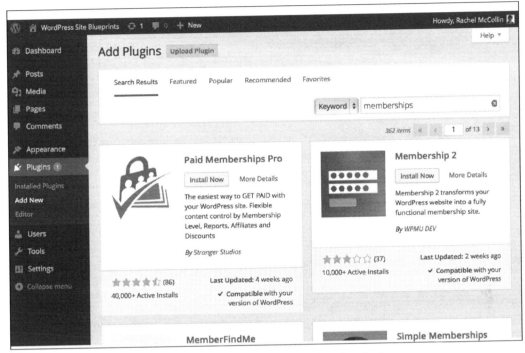

Fig 10.1: Installing the Paid Memberships Pro plugin

3. Click on the **Install Now** button.

4. When the plugin is installed, click on the **Activate** link.

The plugin is installed and ready to go!

Configuring membership settings

Now you need to configure various settings for the plugin. You'll need to add membership levels, create pages for your members to sign up and log in, and view their account and configure payments.

Setting up membership levels

Let's start by creating some membership levels. I'm going to create four tiers of membership for my site:

- **Bronze**: This will be free and give users access to basic content
- **Silver**: This will cost a small amount and give access to more content
- **Gold**: This will cost more with access to more advanced content
- **Platinum**: This will be the most expensive with access to all the site's content, plus support

You might want to use different membership levels for your site and have a different pricing structure. You have a range of options with this plugin; membership can be with a one-off fee, monthly subscription, or an annual subscription. You can set membership to expire after a given period or create a trial period at a lower rate (or for free).

You can set up membership levels using the plugin's setting screens:

1. Go to **Memberships | Membership Levels**.

2. Type in the name of your membership level, a description for it, and a confirmation message that people will see after signing up for it, as shown in the following screenshot:

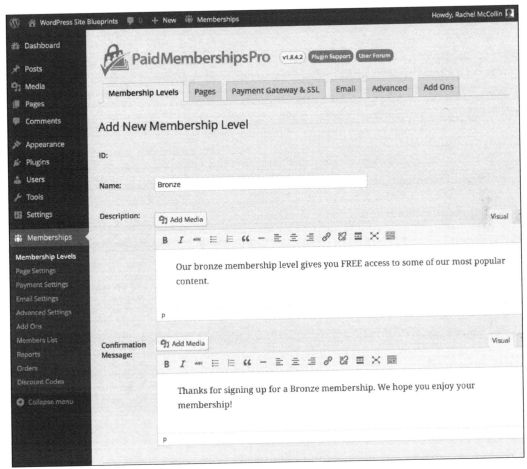

Fig 10.2: Adding a membership level—titles and description

3. Now, scroll down and add payment details, as shown in the following screenshot; this level is free, so I simply type 0.00 in the **Initial Payment** field and leave the **Recurring Subscription** field unchecked:

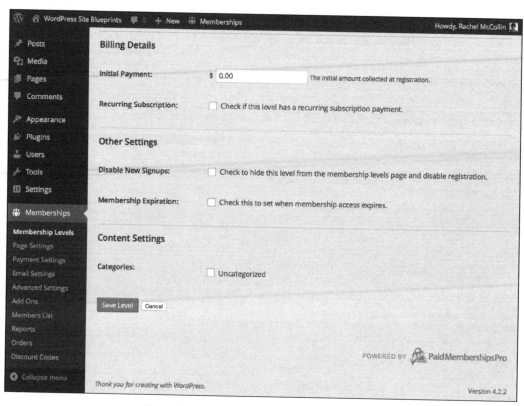

Fig 10.3: Adding a membership level—payments

4. Leave the remaining fields unchecked. This membership level will never expire, so you don't want to disable it, and we aren't using categories to allocate content to membership levels on this site.

 If you're adding membership to an existing site with the content already added, you can use the categories to allocate posts to membership levels. Simply check the relevant categories when setting up your membership levels and ensure that posts are in the appropriate categories. This can save you manually going into all those historical posts and allocating them to a membership level.

5. Now repeat this process for all of your membership levels. The way you set each one up will be very similar, except that the other levels on my site have a subscription payment and a one-month free trial. You can see how I've set this up in the following screenshot:

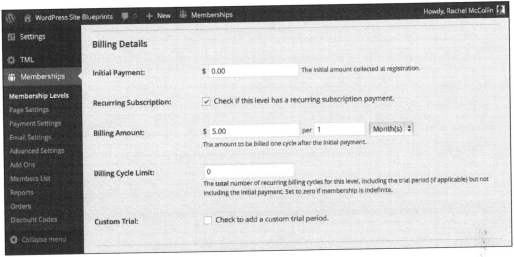

Fig 10.4: Adding a membership level—payments for paid subscriptions

The membership structure I've used is as follows; you could use this or a different structure to suit your site:

- **Bronze**: Free
- **Silver**: Free for the first month and then $5 per month
- **Gold**: Free for the first month and then $10 per month
- **Platinum**: Free for the first month then $15 per month

Once you've done that, you'll have multiple levels registered on your site, as shown in the following screenshot:

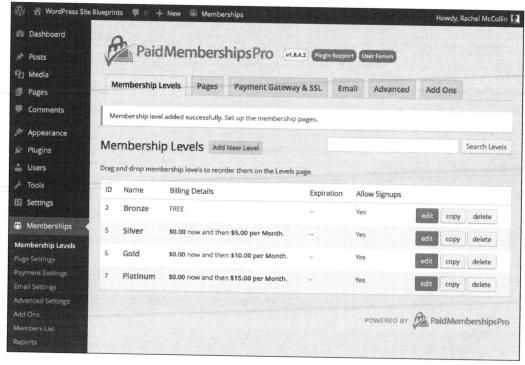

Fig 10.5: The four levels added to the site

Creating pages for membership management

Now that you have levels set up, you need to create some pages for managing your membership system. The plugin will automatically create most of these for you; the only one you have to create yourself (which is optional) is a **Terms of Reference** page. We'll also create a home page and a page for blog posts.

Create three pages for your site in the same way as you'd normally create a page in WordPress:

- **Terms of Reference**: Create this with your site's terms of reference
- **Home**: Create this with some explanatory text (video, images, and more if you have them!)
- **Blog**: You should leave this blank

Now, to create the membership pages, perform the following steps:

1. Go to **Membership | Page Settings**.

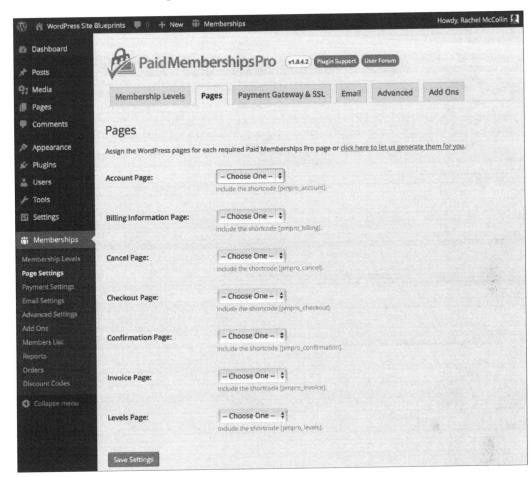

Fig 10.6: The Page Settings screen

2. Click on the link that says **click here to let us generate them for you**.

The plugin will automatically generate the pages for you. You can see them in your main **Pages** listing screen, as shown in the following screenshot; you'll notice that your newly created **Home, Blog,** and **Terms of Reference** pages are there too:

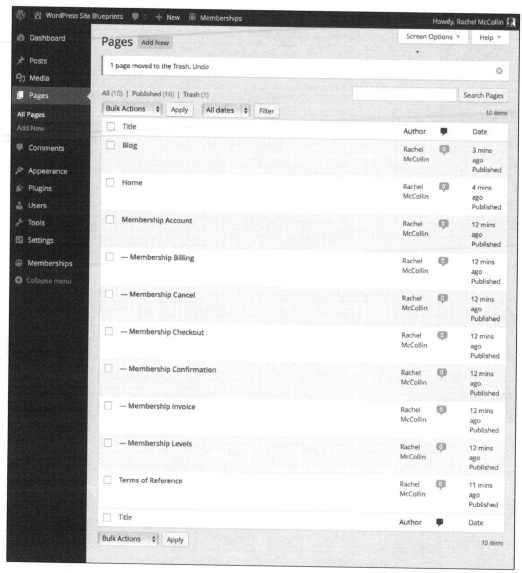

Fig 10.7: Pages for managing memberships

3. Now return to the **Page Settings** screen and select the relevant page for each function in your membership management, as shown in the following screenshot:

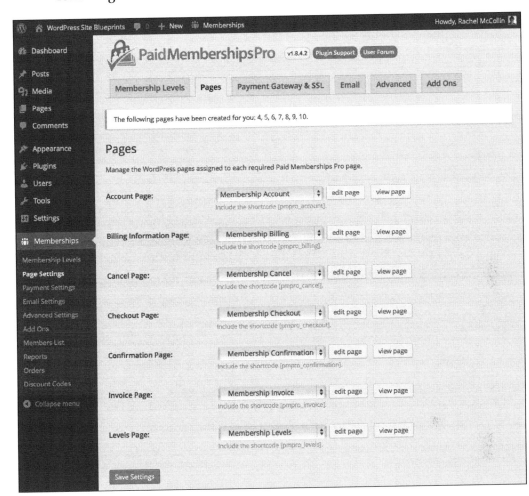

Fig 10.8: Allocating pages for managing memberships

4. Click on the **Save Settings** button to save your changes.

Configuring Payment Settings

The next step is to set up your payment gateway. I'm going to use PayPal.

1. Go to **Membership | Payment Settings**.

2. Complete the fields as shown in Fig 10.9:

     ○ **Payment Gateway**: **PayPal Standard** (or whichever gateway you're using).

     ○ **Gateway Environment**: **Live/Production** (or choose **Sandbox/Testing** if you want to test payments before going live).

     ○ **Gateway Account Email**: The e-mail address associated with your PayPal account.

     ○ **Currency**: Select your currency. I'm using **US Dollars ($)**.

     ○ **Sales Tax**: Enter any sales taxes that apply. I'm leaving this blank.

     ○ **Force SSL**: Select **Yes** if you have an SSL certificate enabled for this site. I don't, so I'm selecting **No**. (An SSL certificate will help to protect your users' data if they are paying for membership or you are storing personal details.)

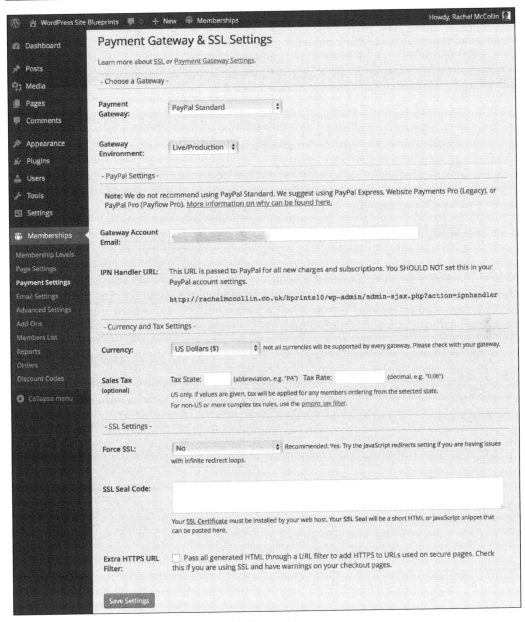

Fig 10.9: Payment Settings

3. Leave the remaining fields as they are and click on the **Save Settings** button.

Configuring Email Settings

Now let's configure e-mail settings for the plugin.

1. Go to **Memberships | Email Settings**.

2. Fill out the fields as follows:

   ° **From Email**: The e-mail address from which any e-mails sent by the system will be sent.

   ° **From Name**: The name you want to appear in the **From** field when someone receives an e-mail from your site.

   ° **Only Filter PMPro Emails?**: Check this if you want e-mail settings to be different for other parts of your site. I'm leaving it unchecked for consistency.

   ° **Send the site admin emails**: Make sure all of the boxes in this section are checked.

   ° **Send members emails**: Uncheck the **New Users** field so that users don't get the default WordPress e-mail as well as the e-mail from the plugin when they register for your site.

3. Finally, click on the **Save Settings** button.

Note that you shouldn't send too many e-mails using this system as it might get you blacklisted as a spammer by your hosting company. If you plan on sending regular outgoing e-mails to your members, talk to your hosting provider about it.

Your settings are shown in the following screenshot:

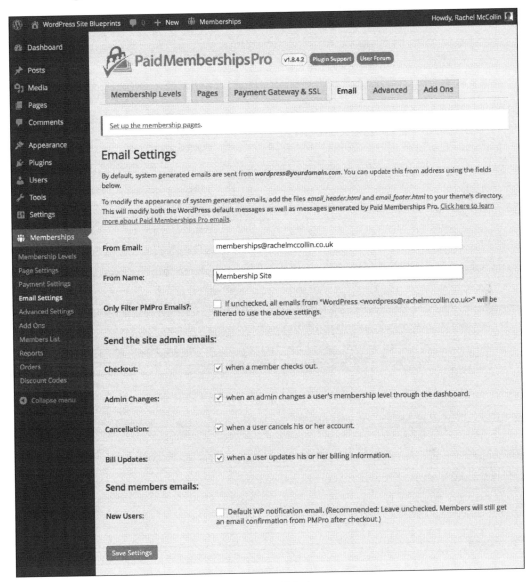

Fig 10.10: Email Settings

Configuring Advanced Settings

Next, let's move on to the **Advanced Settings**:

1. Go to **Memberships | Advanced Settings**.

2. Complete the fields as shown in Fig 10.11:

    ° **Message for Logged-in Non-members**: Leave this as it is or replace it with your own message

    ° **Message for Logged-out Users**: Again, leave this as it is or add your own message if you prefer

    ° **Message for RSS Feed**: You can change this or do as I'm doing and leave it as it is

    ° **Filter searches and archives?**: Select **Yes** so that searches will only return content that the users is allowed access to

    ° **Show Excerpts to Non-Members?**: Select **No**

    ° **Hide Ads from Members?**: This site doesn't include ads, so select **No**

    ° **Use reCAPTCHA?**: Select **No** (reCAPTCHA is a security measure requiring people to type in some text from an image, avoiding the risk of automated spam on your site)

    ° **Require Terms of Reference on signups?**: Select the **Terms of Reference** page that you created earlier

3. Click on **Save Settings** to save your changes.

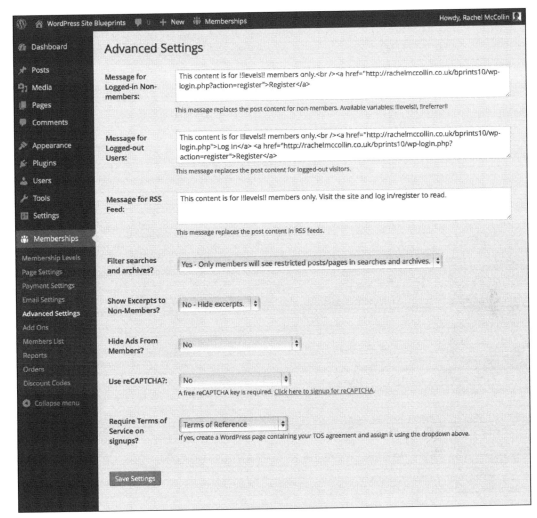

Fig 10.11: Advanced Settings

Configuring Reading Settings

Before starting to add menus and widgets to your site, you need to configure the **Reading Settings**. This isn't part of the plugin's settings screens but a WordPress setting. Follow these steps:

1. In the WordPress admin, go to **Settings | Reading**.
2. In the **Front page displays** section, select the **A static page** radio box.
3. In the **Front page** dropdown, select **Home**.
4. In the **Posts page** dropdown, select **Blog**.
5. Click on the **Save Changes** button.

Here is the **Reading Settings** screen:

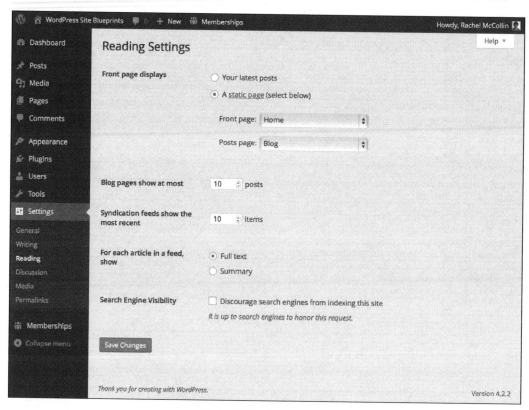

Fig 10.12: Reading Settings

Now it's time to add a navigation menu and some widgets to your site.

Adding a menu and widgets to the site

Now that all of the pages are in place and settings are configured, we can add a navigation menu and some widgets to help users navigate the site. Let's start with a menu.

Creating a navigation menu

Create a menu in the same way you normally would, adding the screens for your membership admin. Follow these steps:

1. In the WordPress admin, go to **Appearance | Menus**.

2. Click on the **create a new menu** link at the top of the screen.

3. To create a new menu, click on the **create a new menu** link, type your menu's name in the **Menu Name** field, and click on the **Create Menu** button, as shown in the following screenshot:

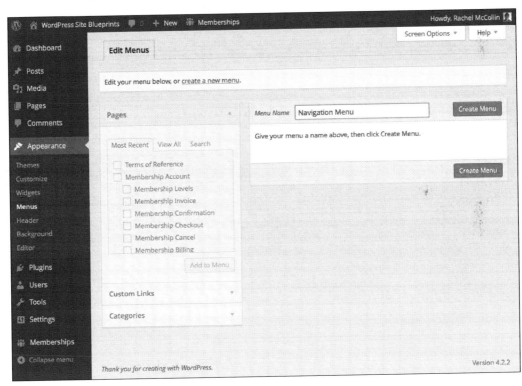

Fig 10.13: Creating a new menu

4. Add the following pages to your menu:
   ○ **Home**
   ○ **Membership Account**
   ○ **Membership Levels**
   ○ **Terms of Reference**
   ○ **Blog**

5. Change the labels for two of the menu items using the **Navigation Label** field, as shown in Fig 10.14.

6. Change **Membership Account** to `Your Account`.

7. Change **Membership Levels** to `Membership Types`.

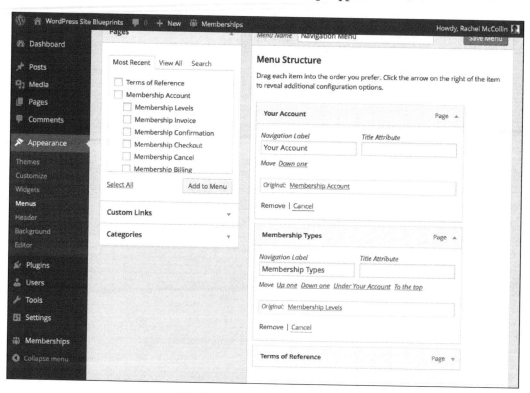

Fig 10.14: Editing navigation labels

8. Once you've added all of the menu items, click on the **Save Menu** button. Yours will look like the following screenshot in the menus admin screen:

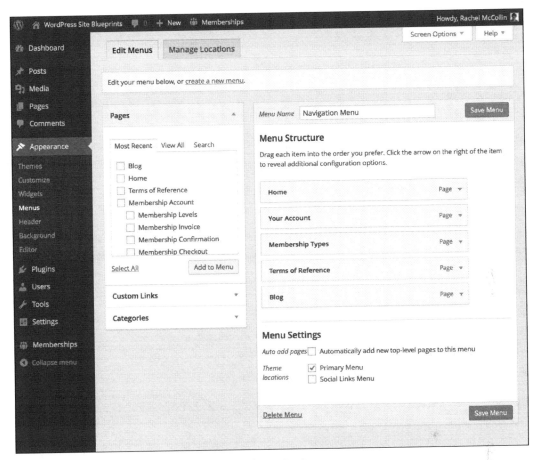

Fig 10.15: The navigation menu

9. Once you've created that menu, create another one in the same way. We'll add this one to a widget shortly. Add these pages to your menu:

   ○ **Terms of Reference**
   ○ **Membership Levels**

10. Call the **Useful Information** menu and save it. You can see it in the following screenshot:

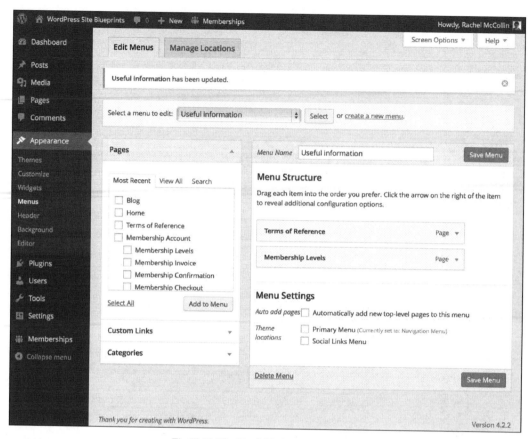

Fig 10.16: The Useful Information menu

Adding widgets

Next, let's add some widgets to help people navigate the site:

1. Go to **Appearance | Widgets**.
2. Add these widgets to the **Sidebar** widget area:
   - **Search**
   - **Recent Posts**
   - **Custom Menu** (select the **Useful Information** menu)

3. Click on **Save** for each widget. You can see the widgets settings screen in the following screenshot:

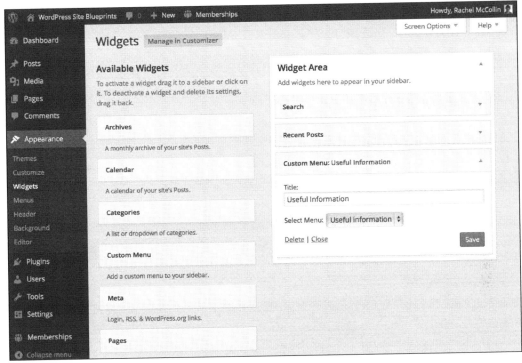

Fig 10.17: The widgets settings screen

So, that's everything set up. Let's start adding some content.

Adding content to your site

The way the plugin works is that it lets you allocate a membership level to each post you create. As our site has hierarchical levels, some posts will need to have more than one level assigned to them, as follows:

- Bronze posts will have all of the membership levels assigned to them, meaning that users with all the membership types will be able to access them
- Silver posts will have the silver, gold, and platinum levels assigned to them
- Gold posts will have gold and platinum levels
- Platinum posts will just have the platinum level

Note that as it's the post you're working with in each case and not the membership level, each post will be visible to people with one or more membership levels. This is is why you take the approach earlier.

> If you want to do things differently, use the post categories instead, creating one for each membership level. Then, assign a single category to each post and assign one or more categories to each membership level in the membership settings. This way you can choose the Gold category for a post, for example, and add the Gold category to each of the Gold and Platinum membership levels. This way you only have to pick your category once for each post and users with a gold or platinum membership will be able to see Gold posts.

Now, you need to add some posts to your site.

To add content to my site, I'm using the data provided by WordPress for theme testing. You can do this by downloading the XML file and following the instructions at `https://codex.wordpress.org/Theme_Unit_Test`. However, your site will probably have more useful content that you've already created or will be creating for it!

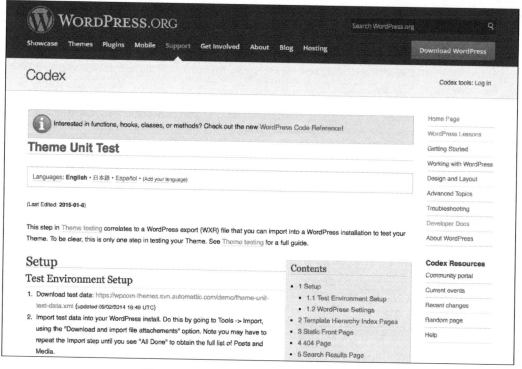

Fig 10.18: The WordPress theme unit testing page

Assigning membership levels to posts

Assigning a membership level to a post is simple. In the post editing screen, check the relevant membership levels in the **Require Membership** metabox, as shown in the following screenshot:

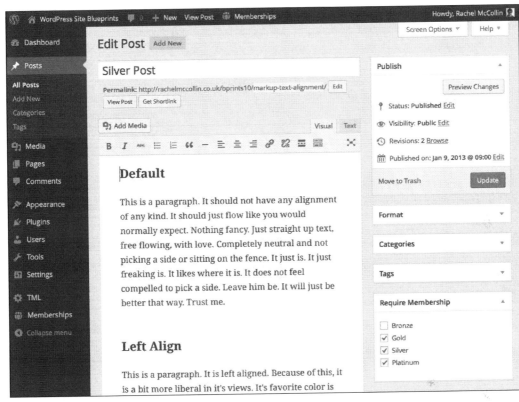

Fig 10.19: Assigning membership levels

The post shown in the preceding screenshot is a Silver post, which means that anyone with a Silver membership or higher will be able to see this. For this reason, I've checked **Silver**, **Gold**, and **Platinum** in the **Require Membership** metabox.

Repeat this with all of your posts: I've set up some dummy posts at various levels, as shown in the following screenshot:

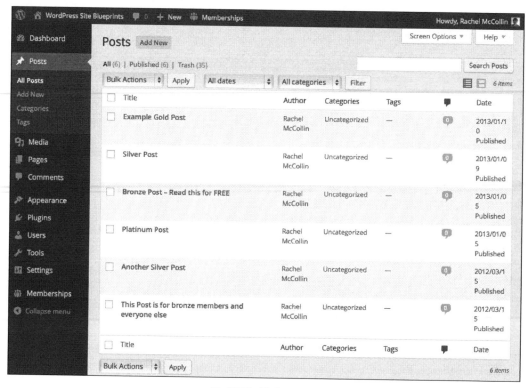

Fig 10.20: All the posts

As all of the posts I've created require at least a Bronze membership account to access them, when someone who isn't a member visits the site, he/she won't see the **Recent Posts** widget in the sidebar because there are no posts for them to see.

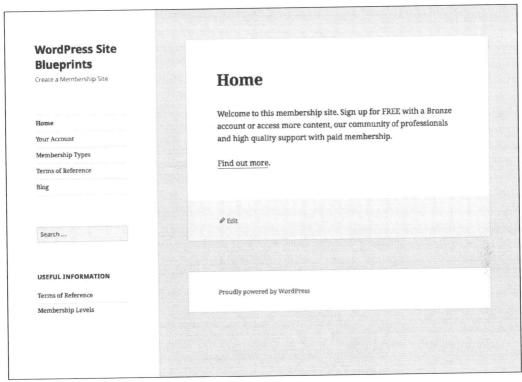

Fig 10.21: Posts are hidden to logged-out users

Registering and accessing content

For users to be able to see the content of our site, they'll need to sign up as members.

The registration screen

The plugin provides you with a page for registering, as shown in the Fig 10.22. Users access this via the **Membership Types** screen, from which they pick the level they want to sign up for.

To register as a member, perform the following steps:

1. First, complete your account details:

Fig 10.22: The registration screen—account details

2. Then, scroll down and check the box under the **Terms of Reference** before clicking on the button to checkout with PayPal:

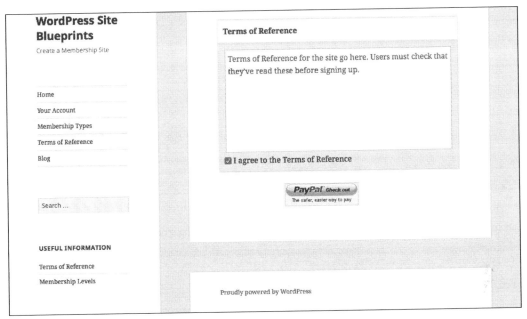

Fig 10.23: The registration screen — Terms of Reference

The plugin takes the content of the **Terms of Reference** page you created and inserts it in the registration page so that people know what they're signing up for.

The user then goes through the process of paying via PayPal and is taken back to a confirmation screen:

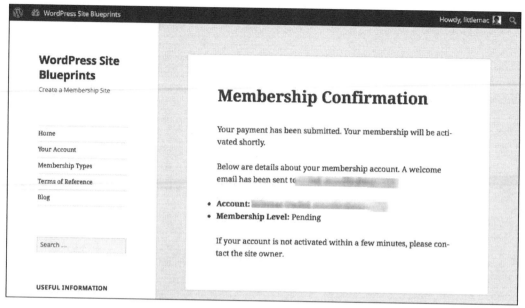

Fig 10.24: The registration confirmation screen

As an administrator, you can see all of the people who have signed up for membership by going to the memberships screen in the WordPress admin, as shown in the following screenshot:

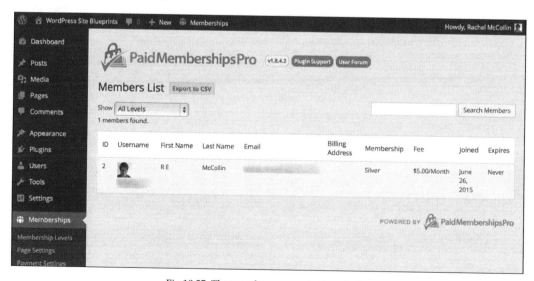

Fig 10.25: The members screen in the admin

Logging in to the site

As members of the public will be using this site, you don't want them to be working in the admin screens at any point. If you directed them to the default WordPress login screen to log in, they would then be taken to their profile screen in the admin, which isn't ideal.

So to avoid this, we'll install another plugin. This plugin is called **Theme My Login**. It lets you create a login page on the frontend of your site and customize it if you want to.

1. Go to **Plugins | Add New**.
2. In the search box, type `theme my login`.
3. Select the **Theme My Login** plugin and click on the **Install Now** button followed by the **Activate** link.
4. The plugin will now be active, and you'll see a TML menu item in the WordPress admin menu.

Before your users can log in, you'll need to edit the settings for the plugin:

1. Click on **TML** in the admin menu.
2. In the general screen that appears, complete the fields as follows:
   ○ **Stylesheet**: Check this box
   ○ **E-mail Login**: Check this box
   ○ **Modules**: Check **Enable AJAX** and **Enable Custom Redirection**
3. Click on the **Save Changes** button.

You can see the settings in the following screenshot:

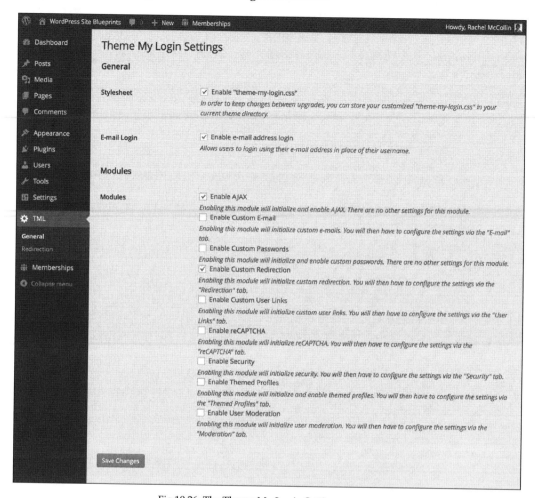

Fig 10.26: The Theme My Login Settings screen

 If you want to be even more secure about your admin pages and completely prevent users from accessing any admin pages by mistake, you can install the **WP Admin No Show** plugin, which is available at `https://wordpress.org/plugins/wp-admin-no-show/`.

As you've enabled redirection, a menu item will appear for this below the **TML** menu in the admin. Use this to set up redirection:

1. Go to **TML | Redirection**.

2. Scroll down to the **Subscriber** metabox, as shown in the following screenshot:

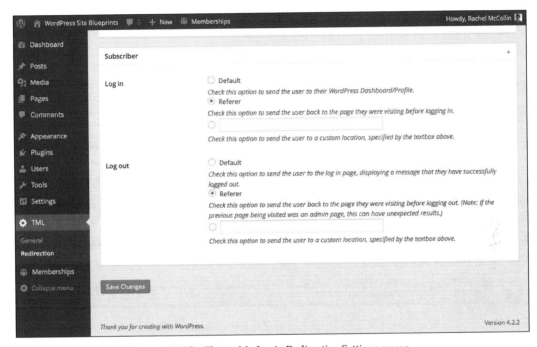

Fig 10.27: The Theme My Login Redirection Settings screen

3. In the **Log in** section, select **Referer**. This will redirect users back to the screen they were on after logging in.

4. In the **Log out** section, select **Referer** again.

5. Click on the **Save Changes** button.

Now, you need to add a link for logging in to your main navigation menu.

1. Go to **Appearance | Menus**.

2. Select your main navigation menu.

3. Add the **Log In** screen to your menu. Don't add the **Log Out** screen, as if a user is logged in, the **Log In** link will automatically change to **Log Out**.

4. Click on the **Save Menu** button.

You can see the new menu in the following screenshot:

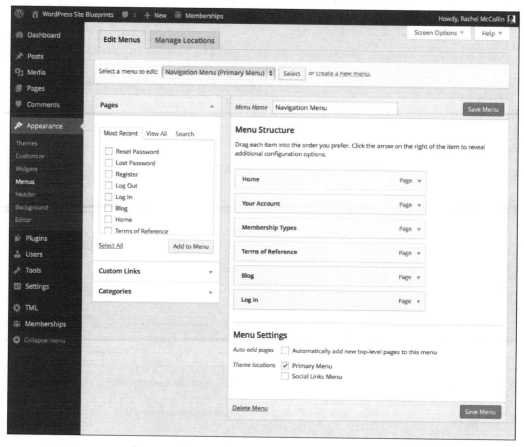

Fig 10.28: The navigation menu with a login page added

Now, when someone clicks on that **Log In** link, they'll get a login screen on your site's frontend, as shown in the following screenshot:

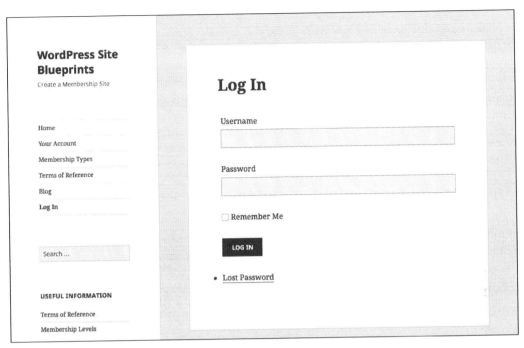

Fig 10.29: The frontend login screen

Here's how the site looks now to a logged-in user:

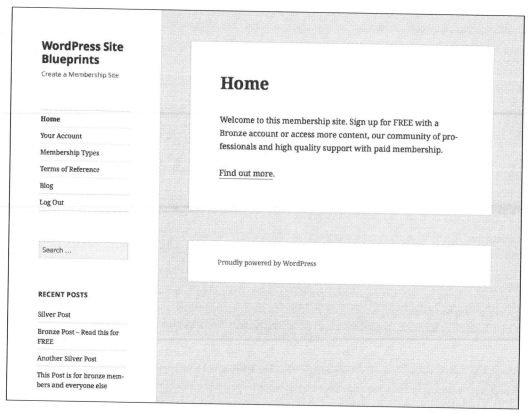

Fig 10.30: The site's frontend as a Silver member would see it

The preceding screenshot is what is seen by a Silver member. In the **Recent Posts** menu in the sidebar, you can only see Bronze and Silver posts. If a Platinum member were to log in, for example, he/she would be able to see more.

Summary

In this chapter, you learned how to create a membership site with multiple membership levels. Specifically, you learned how to install the Paid Memberships Pro plugin. You added four membership levels. You configured membership settings, including payment gateway, e-mail, and more. You also created pages for managing membership and displaying content. You added membership pages to your main navigation and widget areas and created content, which is restricted to certain membership levels. You also added a login screen using the Theme My Login plugin.

Well done! As you can see, WordPress makes it very easy to create a membership site and restrict content to people who have signed up for it and paid for it, and it costs you nothing to set up.

That's the final project in this book. If you've worked through these projects, you should have plenty of inspiration for your own site and your own projects. Whether you're creating a site for yourself, for friends and family, for your employer, or an organization you work or volunteer for, you'll now know how to create a multitude of different kinds of site. WordPress makes it easy, and it's all free! Good luck with your site creation, and I hope this book helps you make something that gives you and your users a lot of pleasure.

Index

Thank you for buying
WordPress 4.0 Site Blueprints
Second Edition

About Packt Publishing

Packt, pronounced 'packed', published its first book, *Mastering phpMyAdmin for Effective MySQL Management*, in April 2004, and subsequently continued to specialize in publishing highly focused books on specific technologies and solutions.

Our books and publications share the experiences of your fellow IT professionals in adapting and customizing today's systems, applications, and frameworks. Our solution-based books give you the knowledge and power to customize the software and technologies you're using to get the job done. Packt books are more specific and less general than the IT books you have seen in the past. Our unique business model allows us to bring you more focused information, giving you more of what you need to know, and less of what you don't.

Packt is a modern yet unique publishing company that focuses on producing quality, cutting-edge books for communities of developers, administrators, and newbies alike. For more information, please visit our website at www.packtpub.com.

About Packt Open Source

In 2010, Packt launched two new brands, Packt Open Source and Packt Enterprise, in order to continue its focus on specialization. This book is part of the Packt Open Source brand, home to books published on software built around open source licenses, and offering information to anybody from advanced developers to budding web designers. The Open Source brand also runs Packt's Open Source Royalty Scheme, by which Packt gives a royalty to each open source project about whose software a book is sold.

Writing for Packt

We welcome all inquiries from people who are interested in authoring. Book proposals should be sent to author@packtpub.com. If your book idea is still at an early stage and you would like to discuss it first before writing a formal book proposal, then please contact us; one of our commissioning editors will get in touch with you.

We're not just looking for published authors; if you have strong technical skills but no writing experience, our experienced editors can help you develop a writing career, or simply get some additional reward for your expertise.

WordPress Responsive Theme Design

ISBN: 978-1-78528-845-6   Paperback: 228 pages

Develop and customize your very own responsive WordPress themes quickly and efficiently

1. Structured learning for new developers and technical consultants to enable you to build responsive WordPress themes.

2. Concise and easy-to-follow walkthroughs of WordPress, PHP, and CSS code.

3. Packed with examples and key tips on how to avoid potential pitfalls.

WordPress Web Application Development
Second Edition

ISBN: 978-1-78217-439-4   Paperback: 404 pages

Build rapid web applications with cutting-edge technologies using WordPress

1. Develop rapid web applications using the core features of WordPress.

2. Explore various workaround techniques to prevent maintenance nightmares by identifying the limitations of WordPress.

3. A practical guide filled with real-world scenarios that will guide you through how to build modular and scalar applications.

Please check **www.PacktPub.com** for information on our titles

WordPress Web Application Development

ISBN: 978-1-78328-075-9   Paperback: 376 pages

Develop powerful web applications quickly using cutting-edge WordPress web development techniques

1. Develop powerful web applications rapidly with WordPress.

2. Practical scenario-based approach with ready-to-test source code.

3. Learn how to plan complex web applications from scratch.

WordPress 3.7 Complete
Third Edition

ISBN: 978-1-78216-240-7   Paperback: 404 pages

Make your first end-to-end website from scratch with WordPress

1. Learn how to build a WordPress site quickly and effectively.

2. Find out how to create content that's optimized to be published on the Web.

3. Learn the basics of working with WordPress themes and playing with widgets.

Please check **www.PacktPub.com** for information on our titles

Made in the USA
San Bernardino, CA
27 September 2015